DO YOU KNOW WHAT I HAVE DONE TO YOU?

What True Love Really Is

PAUL W. SYLTIE

DO YOU KNOW WHAT I HAVE DONE TO YOU?

What True Love Really Is

PAUL W. SYLTIE

Xulon Press
2301 Lucien Way #415
Maitland, FL 32751
407.339.4217
www.xulonpress.com

Paperback ISBN-13: 978-1-66286-460-5
Hard Cover ISBN-13: 978-1-66286-461-2
Ebook ISBN-13: 978-1-66286-462-9

DO YOU KNOW WHAT I HAVE DONE TO YOU?

What True Love Really Is

PAUL W. SYLTIE

Table of CONTENTS

PREFACE

DO YOU KNOW WHAT I HAVE DONE TO YOU?

This short sentence from John 13:12 speaks volumes, but the full meaning has escaped me until quite recently. Now I think I understand it, at least intellectually, and it holds the key to our relationship with Him which He needed to leave record of before He was crucified … in fact, just a matter of hours before He was crucified.

Jesus had just washed the feet of the disciples — which must have amazed and perplexed them — even Peter's feet, while he protested, saying, "Lord, are You washing my feet?" (John 13:6).

Jesus answered by saying, "What I am doing you do not understand now, but you will know after this" (John 13:7).

Peter protested vehemently, "You shall never wash my feet," to which Jesus replied, "If I do not wash you, you have no part of Me" (John 13:8).

In verse 7 Jesus told Peter emphatically that he would not understand what was happening by foot washing, for Peter did not yet have the spirit of God by which love can be comprehended, a love that is intimately entwined with humility ... without which a person cannot comprehend the Father.

"'For all things My hand has made,
And all these things exist,' says the Lord.
'But to this one will I look:
On him who is poor and of a contrite spirit,
And who trembles at My word'" (Isaiah 66:2).

Peter also did not understand the meaning of water itself, not just to wash away the filth and grime from a day's journey along the roads of Israel, but to wash away the dirt and sin of our former lives — about which Peter, a few weeks later, spoke of so eloquently:

"Repent, and let every one of you be baptized in the name of Jesus Christ for the remission of sins, and you shall receive the gift of the holy spirit" (Acts 2:38).

Peter did not understand what was being done to him by the Creator of the earth and all that is in it (Colossians 1:16; John 1:3), for such truth is spiritually discerned and he had no such spirit, as further evidenced by the squabble that erupted amongst the disciples a few minutes later. Luke 22:24-27 makes this fact clear.

"Now there was also a dispute among them, as to which of them should be considered the greatest. And He said to them, 'The kings of the gentiles exercise Lordship over them, and those who exercise authority over them are called benefactors. But not so among you; on the contrary, he who is greatest among you, let him be as the younger, and he who governs as he who serves. For who is greater, he who sits at the table or he who serves? Is it not he who sits at the table? Yet I am among you as the One who serves.'"

Let us return to John 13, verses 13 to 16, which clarifies the meaning of the foot washing and flows naturally into the argument the disciples had in Luke 22.

"You call Me Teacher and Lord, and you say well, for so I am. If then, your Lord and Teacher, has washed your feet, you also ought to wash one another's feet. For I have given you an example, that you should do as I have done to you. Most assuredly, I say to you, a servant is not greater than his master, nor is he who is sent greater than he who sent him. If you know these things, blessed are you if you do them."

If then, your Lord and Teacher, has washed your feet, you also ought to wash one another's feet. For I have given you an example, that you should do as I have done to you (John 13:14).

What? He was the Savior getting down onto the dirty floor and washing the disciples' feet! He was in a literal sense placing Himself below them, in the position of a lowly servant: He in no way during this demonstration showed Himself to be somehow superior or ruler over them. Rather, HE SHOWED THEM HE WAS THEIR SERVANT DESPITE HIM BEING THE CREATOR OF ALL, AND THEIR SAVIOR, THE MESSIAH, THE "I AM"!

Was this just an illustration of how they were to treat one another, or did He literally place Himself below them as a humble servant to them? The answer is obvious. Christ would not lie to anyone, and when He, as Lord and Teacher, kneeled or squatted on the floor and washed their feet, he indeed meant that HE DID NOT CONSIDER HIMSELF TO BE IN ANY WAY SUPERIOR TO THEM. Jesus Christ by this foot washing showed that the ways of the world, where the kingly hierarchy places some people above other people, is a sham, a great evil. The world's hierarchical system is not the system of government amongst the elect, where the least is greatest and the servant of others is the greatest. Jesus Christ in His total humility turns the world's concept of government upside down, confirmed a second time in Philippians.

"Do nothing through strife or vainglory, but in humility let each regard his neighbor better than himself.... Let this mind be in you which was also in Jesus Christ" (Philippians 2:3, 5).

That places us as God's people in a rather awkward position if we still adhere to corporate church organizations, where a corporate hierarchy demands obedience of the ministers and pastors "below" them in the structure, rather than allow the spirit of the Eternal to reign supreme, to have us wash one another's feet as Christ did. To follow the dictates of Christ we must never place another person between us and the Father (Romans 8:26-27; Matthew 6:9). GOD NEVER INTENDED THAT MEN RULE OVER MEN, BUT RATHER THAT HE MUST BE SUPREME ... yet that supremacy is not the authoritarian rulership of men over men. That is Satan's ploy. Therein lies the understanding of true love, being servants to one another even as Christ washed the disciple's feet, and the Father likewise washes our feet. We must in the same vein wash the feet of both the Father and Christ.

But there is another major point in this foot washing scenario that we must not miss. Notice in John 13:2 that, while Satan had already convinced Judas to betray Jesus, Judas was still there at the Passover meeting, and Jesus washed his feet along with those of the other eleven disciples. The meaning? We must wash the feet of even our worst enemies, just as the Eternal shows us in Matthew 5:38-48 and Romans 12:17-21. At

*W*e are those disciples whose feet Jesus Christ is washing!
Let that truth sink in as you read the chapters of this book.

least we should do good to them and not utterly detest and hate them, for that would be murder (I John 3:15). Perhaps even Judas will be raised in a resurrection to life, for God wills that none be lost (II Peter 3:9), even though Jesus stated it would be better that Judas had never been born (Matthew 26:24).

Yet another point of these few verses of John 13 we must not miss. Recall that in John 13:8 Jesus said, in answer to Peter's opposition to having Him wash his feet, "If I do not wash you, you have no part with Me." What exactly is Jesus telling Peter? Is He not saying that unless you let Me serve you, just as I am serving you by washing your feet, that you cannot participate amongst My disciples, whom you also must serve? How is it possible to fulfill God's commands to love one another unless you place yourself below them, as a humble servant, as Jesus was doing that very moment to Peter?

The Greek word for *part* in verse 8 is *meros* (μέρος)[2], meaning "part, portion, or share." It would be impossible for Peter — much less any of the elect — to know and become like the Savior without stooping down to wash the filth

from his brother's feet ... become a servant to him and buoy him up as the Father and Christ do all the time for us. To become a part of the brotherhood is to think, speak, and act as the Father and Christ do ... to become one with them. We must do this for one another within the ecclesia, just like Jesus and the Father are doing for us, in the pattern of John 17:20-21:

> "My prayer is not for them alone. I pray also for those who will believe in me through their message, that all of them may be one, Father, just as you are in me and I am in you. May they also be in us so that the world may believe that you have sent me."

Perhaps now you can see why I chose this title, "Do You Know What I Have Done to You?" as the title of this book. This one statement more than any other — what it portrays in the washing of one another's feet — reveals what true love really is.

WE ARE THOSE DISCIPLES WHOSE FEET JESUS CHRIST IS WASHING! Let that truth sink in as you read the chapters of this book.

INTRODUCTION

JESUS CHRIST'S REVELATION OF LOVE

The concept of "love" is so central to our day-to-day living that we may not even recognize its many facets. Jesus Christ went to great lengths to explain just what love is. He approached it from several viewpoints of get the concept across, and I have discovered ten basic approaches that He used to reveal to us what love is. I call them the "Ten Branches of Love."

Please keep in mind that each of these branches is inextricably intertwined with the others; they cannot be separated, but because they are interrelated it is immensely helpful to break love into its parts, examine each part separately, and then reassemble them to give a more complete understanding of the whole.

We need to understand that the message of "love" has been the most maligned and misunderstood concept in all of human history. Yet it is the most important focus of our very existence, for it is because of our

THE EARTH AND VINE AND BRANCHES OF LOVE[1]

Creator's love that we are even here. Would it not make sense, then, that Satan the Devil would do everything in his power to confuse the meaning and practice of love amongst all humans, especially the ecclesia? Indeed, the Adversary has done a remarkable job of confusing our understanding of love, so we must explore just what we are missing and regain the truth that has been lost. With God's spirit we can do this, but without that spirit we cannot, for "… the spirit reveals all things, yes, the deep things of God" (I Corinthians 2:10).

Definitions of Love

We need to first delve into God's word to discover the meaning of love as used in its various contexts in both the Old and New Testaments.

Old Testament[2]

Ahab. "To love or like; basically to have a strong emotional attachment to, and a desire to either possess or be in the presence of the object." In various contexts the word is used as follows:

- The love of a man for a woman, or a woman for a man, which is rooted in sexual desire but, as a rule, a desire within the bounds of lawful relationships, like Isaac and Rebekah (Genesis 24:67)
- An erotic but legal love outside of marriage, with a desire to marry and care for that person, like Shechem and Dinah (Genesis 34:1)

- In a few cases an inordinate desire for sexual relations (II Samuel 13:1)
- Marriage without the presence of love for the partner (Genesis 29:30)
- Usually does not connote "making love," which is the Hebrew word *yada*, "to know," or *shakab*, "to lie with," but in a few cases it can mean so as with Solomon and his wives (I Kings 11:1)
- Signifies with whom one has made or intends to make love (Jeremiah 20:20)
- The love between parents and their children, as Abraham's love for his son Isaac (Genesis 22:2)
- The close attachment of a daughter-in-law to a mother-in-law, as Ruth and Naomi (Ruth 4:15), or of a servant to his master (Exodus 21:5)
- The seeking of a relationship to others according to God's laws

Other Hebrew words for love such as *ohab* and *ahabah* are derived from the same root as *ahab*. Two other Hebrew words are translated as love: *dowd* ("to love, lover, friend"), and *rayah* ("beloved companion or bride").

New Testament[3]

Agape. "The attitude of God toward His Son (John 17:26), the human race (John 3:16; Romans 5:8), and believers in Christ (John 14:2)," with many attributes depending on the context, as follows.

- His will toward His children concerning their attitudes toward one another and towards all men. (John 13:34; I Thessalonians 3:12; II Peter 1:7)
- His desire for His children to express His nature (I John 4:8)
- Known by the actions it motivates through understanding the gift of His Son (I John 4:9-10)
- Its perfect expression as seen in Christ (II Corinthians 5:14; Ephesians 2:4)
- A major fruit of the spirit of God (Galatians 5:22)
- God is its primary object in obedience to His commandments (John 14:15; I John 5:3)
- Not an impulse from the feelings and emotions towards brethren or anyone, and does not always follow one's natural inclinations, or spend itself only on those for whom some affinity is discovered; it seeks the welfare of all (Romans 15:2), works no ill to anyone (Romans 13:8-10), and seeks opportunity to do good to anyone, but especially to the ecclesia (Galatians 6:10)
- Expresses a deep and constant love and interest of a perfect Being towards entirely unworthy objects, producing a reverential love towards God, and a desire to help others seek Him

The word *agapao* means essentially the same as agape.

Phileo. "To be a friend to or have an affection toward, but never as a command for men to love God."

- Cherishing God above all else (John 21:17)
- To love life, though this idea met Jesus' reproof (John 12:25)
- Tender affection (I Peter 3:10)

Other words in Greek in the New Testament mean similar things, coming from the same Greek root, such as *Philadelphia*, *philadelphos*, and *philanthropia*.

Another Greek word, not used in the New Testament, is *eros*, which means "sexual love or passion," that was defined by Plato as physical attraction that refines itself in terms of appreciation of the beauty within the person, even without an erotic physical attraction, called "platonic love."

Other Greek words for love are *storge* ("love or affection"), *philautia* ("self-love"), and *xenia* ("hospitality").

God *Is* Love

God is love. It is who and what He is.

"Beloved, let us love one another, for love is of God; and everyone who loves is *born* [*gennao*, "begotten"][4] of God and knows God. He who does not love does not know God, for *God is love*. In this the love of God was manifested towards us, that God has sent His only begotten Son into the world, that we might live through Him" (I John 4:7-9; emphasis mine).

God is love. How can we know God? By knowing what love is, amongst the many other things that God is. Indeed, Paul makes clear just how critical love is, greater even than faith and hope, as major as they are: "And now abide faith, hope, love, these three; but the greatest of these is love" (I Corinthians 13:13).

Love is so critical to knowing God … and we all are on a crusade to know Him better and better each day, or we should be. Knowing love is so crucial that Solomon wrote in Song of Solomon 8:6,

"Wear me as a seal close to your heart,
Wear me as a ring upon your hand;
For love is strong as death itself,
And passion masters like the grave,
Its flashes burn like flame,
True lightning flashes" (Moffatt Translation; emphasis mine).

Love is strong as death. What a powerful statement!

Along with the truth that God is love comes the emphatic pleading of our Creator to love Him. This desire is repeated in many scriptures concerning Israel and all people of all nations.[5] Let us now search the Scriptures and discover the reality of love in as many contexts as possible, approaching God's love not just from word definitions — though we will begin there — but from the many ways that Jesus Christ expressed love to us in His word. You will be amazed by how thoroughly Jesus exposes the meaning of love if you will but open your eyes and look!

A student concentrates on his homework in a library, preparing for upcoming tests. It is a task that requires time and dedication, while putting away for the moment all other distractions that might interfere with this most critical effort in the life of a student.[1]

THE FIRST BRANCH

LOVE IS IMPLICIT
IN THE TEN COMMANDMENTS

The walk from the dormitory to the library was not a long one, and so pleasant in the gorgeous spring weather of the late semester. John had done well so far at the University of Minnesota, achieving the highest grade point average of anyone in his senior class at the School of Agriculture, Forestry, and Home Economics. He would need to study for several hours this evening to prepare for final exams coming up in just a few days. He was especially concerned about calculus, but through sweat and not a few tears he had made it through the first two semesters of this make-or-break class.

On the way to the exit door he passed by the girls' wing and waiting room sofas. Several cute girls sat in a semi-circle, chattering up a storm … rather scantily clad, as if inviting a further look. Books in hand, he passed by them quickly so as not to draw their attention or be tempted to dwell on their wanton invitations.

Out the door and onto the sidewalk he strode, assembling in his mind the work cut out for him this fine evening. Oh, how beautiful were the songs of robins and warblers, luring his fancy toward the outdoors and natural world. Leaves of elms and ash trees were nearly fully expanded, now overpowering much of the dull gray and brown of concrete, brick, and stone that comprised the sidewalks and stark edifices of the expansive St. Paul campus.

Soon he had walked up the library steps and ascended the marble stairs to the main floor and its myriad of bookshelves, interspersed with small tables and chairs along the peripheral windows, and large tables between stacks of books reaching nearly to the ceiling. He found himself an empty chair in a fairly private area alongside a window, laid out his notes and book, and began reading.

The faint whisper of students a few stacks of books away soon crept into his consciousness. It made him want to join their conversation on more pleasant matters, but the temptation was thrust aside. As the minutes passed his mind drifted to thoughts of the beautiful, fragrant river valley on the home farm. That too he thrust away, and forced himself again to bear into his studies. After all, finals were coming, and the distress of the moment would be well worth the short-term sacrifice of avoiding shop talk with other students, whose objective of being here for many was not to master any academic challenges. So many students squandered their time on senseless diversions and parties; why should they even be here, he thought, if not to use their time wisely?

Two hours passed, and in weariness he collected his books and notes and walked out the door of the library into the florid night air, the lights of the city reflecting on scattered clouds, streetlights painting odd patterns on the sidewalks. A silent couple strolled by on their way to the dorm, which he quickly recognized as his roommate and a girl named Cindy he had been dating. "Nice night," said Gary, seeing his scholarly roommate was calling it quits for the night. "You really raise the curve for these courses — Ha! I'll bet you really love Dr. Mitchell's class."

"Sometimes," John confided, "but it's tough work. I wish there was another way to complete the degree; they make it so hard on us!"

The three of them trooped up the grade to the dormitory. It had been a long day, and they were more than ready for a good night's sleep. As John and Gary passed through the lobby, and Cindy headed toward the girls' wing, a few fellows were seen hanging around the vending machine, sharing some expletives that both John and Gary had to close their minds to. It was late, and they both knew nothing good happens after midnight.[2]

This story, synthesized from my days of undergraduate work at the University of Minnesota,[3] may seem simple and bland, but it points toward a major fact of life: the Ten Commandments are applicable and intrinsic in everything that we do. Take a deeper look at this very short story and see how all the commandments are moving through it.[4]

Commandment 1. You shall have no other Gods before me. Throughout this evening the intent was to serve the living God, even though John was a young man.

Commandment 2. You shall make no graven images. Though John was tempted to place the natural world that beckoned to him before his studies, he stifled that desire and went on to study.

Commandment 3. You shall not take God's name in vain. He steeled his mind against the expletives of others who used God's name in vain.

Commandment 4. Remember the Sabbath day to keep it holy. John dutifully was working on one of the six days of the week; when the Sabbath arrived, his plan was to rest from this studies.

Commandment 5. Honor your father and mother. His father had emphatically set the example to work hard at whatever he set his hand to do; he honored that example and was not about to squander the evening's responsibilities.

Commandment 6. You shall not murder. Though some students in the library were a distraction due to their whispering, John refused to hate them for their disrespect of those needing silence, but concentrated all the more. To hate your brother is akin to murder (I John 3:15).

Commandment 7. You shall not commit adultery. There were strong temptations to look upon those cute dormitory girls with lust, but he kept his desires under control. To lust after a woman is likened to committing adultery (Matthew 5:28).

Commandment 8. You shall not steal. Many other pastimes could be pursued rather than studying for exams that evening, and they would have been more pleasurable, but that would be stealing time from the foremost occupation of the moment: studying for exams.

Commandment 9. You shall not bear false witness. When asked by his roommate about Dr. Mitchell's class, John did not sugar coat his response but told the truth of how he felt about it.

Commandment 10. You shall not covet. Though studying is hard work, he did not allow his desire to wander among the trees and birds to distract him from the important work at hand.

All of these commandments relate to what we do every day, each person in slightly different ways. They are intrinsic to all that we do, say, and think, and they all relate to how we interact with our fellow man … how we show love to those around us.

Jesus was asked by a lawyer, "Teacher, which is the great commandment of the law?" His answer drove directly towards the Ten Commandments, and expressly in terms of love!

"Jesus said to him, 'You shall love the Lord your God with all your heart, with all your soul, and with all your mind. This is the first and great commandment. And the second is like it: You shall love your neighbor as yourself. On these two commandments hang all the Law and the Prophets'" (Matthew 22:36-40).

This is a reiteration of Deuteronomy 6:1-9, where Moses wrote that the commandments, statutes, and judgments of Yahweh Elohim were to be kept so the Israelites might enjoy a long life, and that they might "… love the Lord your God with all your heart, with all your soul, and with all your might" (verse 5). In every case the word love (Hebrew *ahab*)[6] is used to describe the commandments.

Jesus defined all of the commandments in terms of love to God (the first four) and love to neighbor (the last six), and in fact defined love to one's Creator and to one's neighbor as encompassing the entire meaning of the Law

Jesus proclaimed a message that resonated profoundly with those who were called to be His disciples. Where else could they turn, but to the One who had the answers to their deepest-seated questions?[5]

and the Prophets … the writings of the Old Testament that we possess in our homes today! A major portion of Jesus' teaching was revealed when He sat down on the Mount of Olives and taught his disciples: "Therefore, whatever you want men to do to you, do also to them, for this is [the meaning of] the Law and the Prophets" (Matthew 7:12).

Therefore, we can say without a doubt that the essence and meaning of the Laws of God are love … love in its many and varied contexts. In fact, the Scriptures emphatically say so.

"For this is the love of God, that we keep His commandments, and His commandments are not grievous" (I John 5:3).

"If you love Me, keep My commandments …. He that has My commandments, and keeps them, he it is that loves Me; and he that loves Me shall be loved of My Father, and I will love him and will manifest Myself to him …. If a man loves Me, he will keep My words, and the Father will love him, and We will come unto him and make Our abode with him" (John 14:15, 21, 23).

"If you keep My commandments you shall abide in My love, even as I have kept My Father's commandment, and abide in His love" (John 15:10).

"And this is love, that we walk after His commandments. This is the commandment, that as you have heard from the beginning you should walk in it" (II John 1:6).

This "yoke" of commandment keeping, as Jesus indicated, is not burdensome, for He Himself said,

"Come unto Me, all you who labor and are heavy-laden and I will give you rest. Take My yoke upon you and learn of Me, for I am meek and lowly of heart, and you shall find rest unto your souls. For My yoke is easy, and My burden is light" (Matthew 11:28-30).

This is the same "easy burden" that Micah recorded in Micah 6:8: " … what is good, and what does the Lord require of you but to walk justly, to love mercy, and to walk humbly with your God?"

Some detractors to the laws of God will contend that somehow these laws, which are not burdensome and show love to God and neighbor, are no longer in force. However, Jesus Himself in the Sermon on the Mount, immediately after stating the Beatitudes, made clear that He did not come to destroy the Law and the Prophets, but rather to fulfill them (Matthew 5:17). The word *fulfill* is from the Greek *pleroo*, meaning "to fill,"[7] like to fill a net (Matthew 13:48), fill a building (John 12:3), fill a city (Acts 5:28), or fulfill needs (Philippians 4:19). The word is used figuratively also as a measure of iniquity (Matthew 23:32), of people in the body of Christ (Ephesians 1:23; Colossians 2:10), of Christ Himself, and of believers with the spirit (Ephesians 5:18).

When Jesus came to earth and lived as a human being, He was the embodiment of righteousness and did not sin (Hebrews 4:15). Moreover, the spirit that has been placed within the elect at baptism and the laying on of hands (Acts 2:38) codes for the very laws that were first written on tables of stone; they are now written on "tables of flesh" within the hearts of the elect (II Corinthians 3:2) so they are able to live by expressing fruits of that spirit (Galatians 5:22-23) in their daily living. Jesus Christ came to reveal through His living how the Law is to be kept in the spirit, as an example for each one of us.

"For this is the covenant that I will make with the house of Israel after those days, says the Lord: I will put My laws in their mind and write them on their hearts; and I will be their God, and they shall be My people" (Hebrews 8:10; see Jeremiah 31:33).

The "new commandment" that Jesus gave the disciples in John 13:34, "That you love one another; as I have loved you, that you also love one another," is not a literal new commandment to add to the original ten, but a command to love in "newness or freshness" (Greek, *kainos*),[8] especially of that which is unaccustomed or unused, not new as being recent, but new in

form and quality, of a different nature contrasted to the old ways. Jesus Christ took the Ten Commandments and refreshed the meaning and application of them in their spiritual intent, showing through His life and words what it truly means to worship no idols, not take the Father's name in vain, honor your parents, not kill, not

I will put my laws in their mind and write them on their hearts; and I will be their God, and they shall be My people (Hebrews 8:10).

commit adultery, not steal, not bear false witness, and not covet. This renewed understanding of the law has always existed, but has been suppressed in daily living within Satan's world, and is now unveiled through the indwelling spirit of the elect. If ever there was love shown to the elect by the Creator, this was it … to reveal how each of us must walk in the footsteps of Jesus Christ, our Elder Brother (Romans 8:29; I John 2:6), to keep His laws, commandments, statutes, and judgments just as Abraham, the father of the faithful, did (Genesis 26:5; Romans 4:11-13).

The very covenants Yahweh made with Abraham, Isaac, and Jacob, and later with the nation of Israel, epitomize the love that the Eternal Creator granted to His people, even when they rebelled against Him. These covenants were based on obedience to the laws of Elohim.

Yahweh's covenant with Abraham, Isaac, and Israel. That *agreement* [*briyth*, "league or confederacy, usually with men"][10] involved making a great nation of him, various blessings to his own family and to all the families on earth, and a great name (Genesis 12:1-3). These blessings of the covenant were due to Abraham's obedience to "... My charge, My commandments, My statutes, and My laws" (Genesis 26:5), blessings that were passed on to Isaac and Jacob, and thence to Ephraim, Manasseh, and all of the twelve tribes. Those promises were carried along with the descendants of Israel as they escaped from Egypt to meet the Eternal at Mt. Sinai, where Yahweh proclaimed,

"Now therefore, if you will indeed obey My voice and keep My covenant, then you shall be a special treasure to Me above all people, for all the earth is Mine. And you shall be to Me a kingdom of priests and a holy nation" (Exodus 19:5-6).

What greater love could the Eternal show to the descendants of Abraham than to promise them priesthoodship! We know the infamous end of this proposal which the Israelites had initially said they would follow (Exodus 19:8), with the incident of the golden calf (Exodus 32) and the near-destruction of the whole nation except for the intervention of Moses on their behalf (Exodus 32:10-14). This covenant, that became known as the Melchisedec priesthood, is the very covenant that the Eternal has made with those today in whom He has placed His spirit, those who will indeed inherit eternal life as

Abraham, the father of the faithful, was an amazing patriarch who gave all that he had to follow the Creator, even traveling to a far land without a clear destination in sight. The laws he kept were those of God, and he never wavered in following them all his days.[9]

kingdom priests (Jeremiah 31:33; Hebrews 8:10; Revelation 5:10). This covenant is based on the very laws and statutes observed by Abraham, the father of the faithful (Romans 4:12-13), and observed by God's people today.

Yahweh's covenant with Israel in Moab. Forty years after the giving of the Commandments at Mt. Sinai, Yahweh made another covenant with Israel in Moab, an agreement that is revealed in Deuteronomy 32:24-26.

"So it was, when Moses had completed writing the words of this law in a book, when they were finished, that Moses commanded the Levites, who bore the ark of the covenant of the Lord, saying, 'Take this Book of the Law, and put it beside the ark of the covenant of the Lord your God, that it may be there as a witness against you ....'"

This law may be called the Law of Moses, which was the temporary, ceremonial law of the Old Testament. It regulated the priesthood, sacrifices, feasts, rituals, meat and drink offerings, and so forth, all of which foreshadowed Him and ended at the crucifixion. This law was added "till the seed should come," and that seed was Christ (Galatians 3:16, 19). The rituals and sacrifices of Moses' law pointed forward to Christ's sacrifice. When He died, this law came to an end.[11]

Despite the rebellion and corruption of Israel in their failure to obey the laws of Yahweh, He nevertheless loved these reprobates for the sake of His promises made to Abraham. He would fulfill those promises and, despite their hardheartedness and disobedience, He would still carry out the plan of redemption for mankind after Adam and Eve sinned in the Garden of Eden. His love for them never failed, even though He reprimanded them strongly, and warned of their horrible fate upon failing to follow the Eternal's ways (Leviticus 25; Deuteronomy 28).

The laws of God, implicit with His covenantal relationship with His people, reveal His incredible love and care even for such sinful people. It is a love that encourages them, pleads with them, to turn from their evil ways and enjoy the fruits of righteousness, lawful living, in this age and in the ages to come (II Kings 17:13; Jeremiah 18:8; 25:5; 26:3; Ezekiel 33:11; Daniel 9:13; Jonah 3:8; Zechariah 1:4).

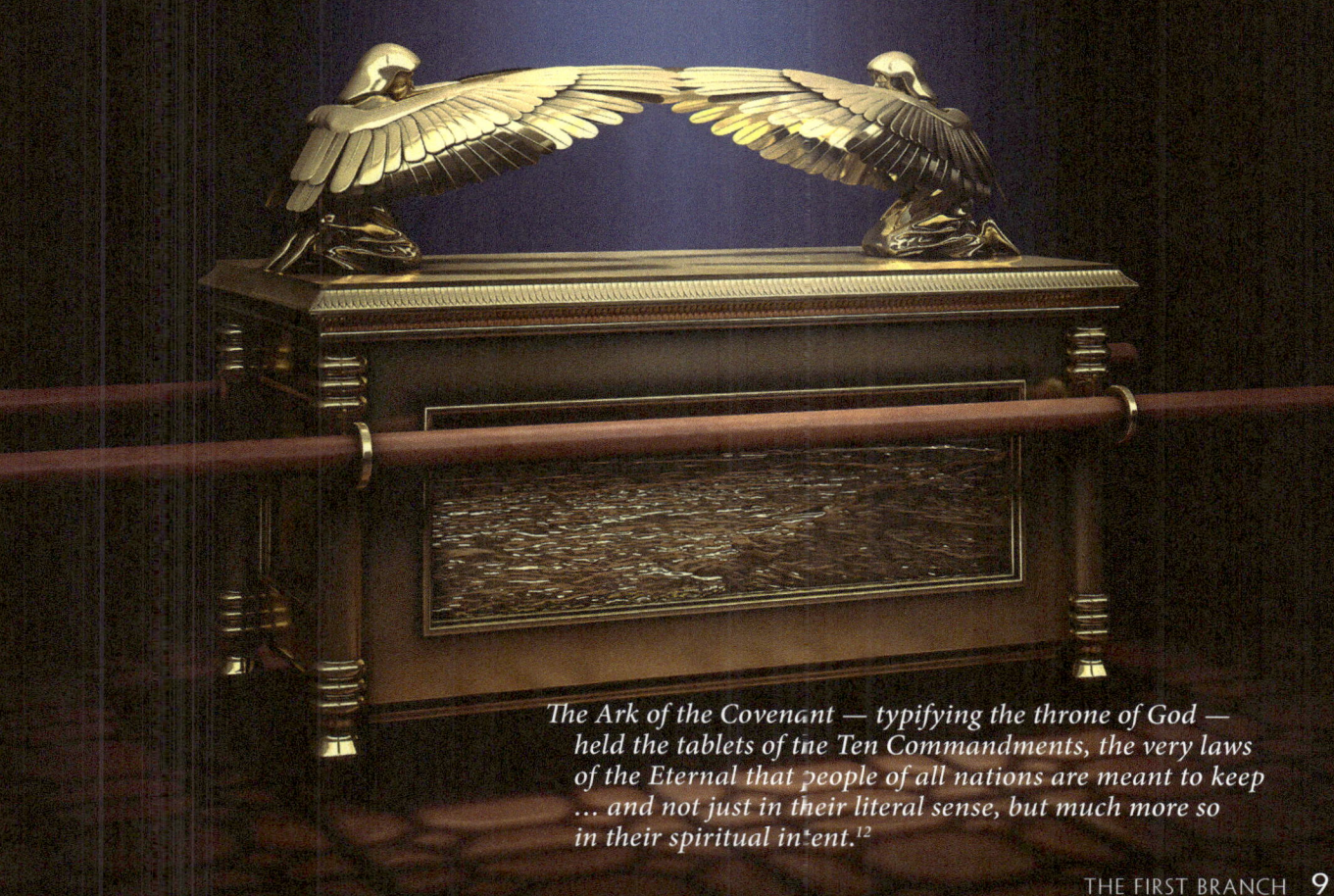

'Take this Book of the Law, and put it beside the ark of the covenant of the Lord your God, that it may be there as a witness against you...' (Deuteronomy 31:26)

The Ark of the Covenant — typifying the throne of God — held the tablets of the Ten Commandments, the very laws of the Eternal that people of all nations are meant to keep ... and not just in their literal sense, but much more so in their spiritual intent.[12]

A young and foolish son of a farmer wants his inheritance right now, not understanding the great responsibility that comes with it … to use wealth wisely for the benefit of one's family and community, and especially for the Creator, to whom a person is ultimately responsible for everything in life.[1]

THE SECOND BRANCH

LOVE IS A
FRUIT OF THE SPIRIT

There was no farmer in all the northern Corn Belt who had prospered more than John Olson. He had seemingly endless fields of corn, wheat, alfalfa, and flax that yielded their bounty every year, and his cattle fed on the lush pastures of the hillier land that were tended by his several hired men. John's barns and grain bins were filled with hay and corn for the winter, and the houses for himself, his children, and his hired help were strong and secure.

He had two sons, Robert and Arne, who helped make his operation the picture book of success. Over a period of time Arne, the youngest son, became unsettled and dissatisfied with the hard work of planting fields, cultivating, cutting and baling hay, and other tasks that no longer satisfied his wanderlust. So, one day he asked his father, "Dad, please give me my share of the inheritance and let me go on my way. I have important things in life I want to experience."

"Well son," said John, "I guess I can give you what is yours, but I am concerned about what you might do on such short notice. Are you sure you won't reconsider?"

"No, dad. I've made up my mind. Let me have what is mine and I will be gone."

Saddened with his son's immature decision, John doled out Arne's portion of the estate, and Arne loaded his pickup truck with his things and, with hardly a kind goodbye to his father, sped down the driveway toward the city of Minneapolis, where some friends were waiting for him. John watched the vehicle turn onto the main county highway and disappear down the road. "Watch over him; keep him safe," he uttered silently to God in the cool morning air.

In a few hours Arne met his friends in the big city, who showed him an apartment they had found for him — a really nice one — and once his things were moved in they celebrated his coming with a bash at a local tavern. So began weeks of wild living: booze, drugs, women, and riotous behavior. It was the life he had dreamed about for several years, freedom from the moral constraints of his parents and family, and release from the rules of the community that surrounded and nurtured him as he grew up from a tiny babe to the strapping, handsome young man he now was.

The weeks flowed into months, and the loose living began to take its toll. He began to feel more and more empty, wondering what the point was of all this reveling that was giving him hangovers and headaches, and above all rapidly depleting his bank balance. Without productive work he was relying solely on the inheritance from his dad, as were his friends who sponged off his largesse as much as they could.

One day Arne was paying for his bill at the bar, but the credit card was rejected: "insufficient funds" was the message. Heart racing, he assured the cashier there must be a mistake … but no, his account was totally drained. Now he would no longer be able to pay his rent, nor afford gas for his vehicle. Things began to look bleak. He would have to work to survive.

Arne could not bear to return to work on the farm; he would have to face his father, but farm work was all he knew … and by now all of his friends had deserted him. Despite the fact that the farm economy was under great distress with low prices for grain and livestock, and sky-high production costs, his best bet was to seek a position somewhere in agriculture. Without money he was suddenly

How wonderful a moment it is when a prodigal son returns to his father and repents of the great evil he has done by squandering the wealth his loving father had saved for him. The message is clear: It is never too late to repent and climb back onto the roadway that leads to Life.

an outcast in the city, so with his last bit of gas he drove out into the farmlands surrounding Minneapolis and stopped at a large livestock operation. Surely there would be work for a young man of his stature and experience.

The manager of the farm greeted him and offered him a position as laborer in the hog operation. "The only position I have available is to help with feeding the pigs; our previous employee just left. Take it or leave it … and, oh yes, we don't pay a lot."

Arne felt he had little choice, so he agreed to take on the job of feeding hogs in the smelly, dirty hog confinement setting, a job he detested but desperately needed to make ends meet. He was offered a small trailer in which to live, and began the daily work of feeding the hogs, sweeping down the alleyways, and performing other menial tasks around the expansive hog operation.

Week after week Arne faithfully fed and cared for the hogs, and week after week his subsistence wages barely allowed him enough money for food and gas. Things were getting desperate, and he began to wonder how he could ever have left such a fine position as a son of his father, working on the home farm where he had plenty to eat, excellent housing, and profitable and honorable work within his home community of family and friends. Now he was captured to these smelly, miserable hogs. "I can't take this anymore. I will return to the home farm and face my father and family, and work as a hired hand. That will be much better than this!"

In the morning Arne loaded his things in his pickup, stopped by the manager's office to give his notice, and slowly drove on back to the home farm several hours away. It was a painful, difficult drive, but it seemed the right thing to do. How was he to survive outside of his father's care at this point. Oh, how he had messed up!

It was mid-afternoon by the time Arne turned on to the county road that led to the home farm. He stopped for a minute on the side of the road, got out, and just stood gazing over the good land of his youth, the cattle grazing on the distant hills and the corn in midsummer tasseling, leaves fluttering in the warm afternoon breeze.

On towards the driveway he slowly drove, turning in just as his father, standing by the machine shed, caught sight of his pickup. Could it be Arne? It is Arne!

In great excitement John ran towards the driveway and met the pickup just as it was about to reach the house. Arne stopped and opened his door, stepped out, and father and son hugged one another for the longest time … a joyous, tear-filled reunion.

Arne said, "Father, I have sinned against heaven and in your sight, and am no longer worthy to be called your son."[3]

… to which John responded, "Bring out the best robe and put it on him, and put a ring on his hand and sandals on his feet. And bring the fatted calf here and kill it, and let us eat and be merry: for this my son was dead and is alive again; he was lost and is found!"[4]

Of course, this is a modern version of the Parable of the Prodigal Son from Luke 15, without the jealous older brother, and I do not know how to conclude the story of the son's return home. What would the father give him nowadays? A new set of clothes, new shoes … certainly a full-course meal in front of all the family, hired men, and community. What an incredible show of love this is, accepting back with untold joy a son who in the world's eyes did not deserve to be readmitted to the family — and certainly not in the eyes of the older brother. Yet, he had repented of his foolish choices. Finally he saw his father's correct teachings and chose to follow them. What an amazing story of love, showing love to be utterly selfless, forgiving, and joyous … a son thought to be dead suddenly appearing out of nowhere, and alive! Is not this the story of each of us at repentance?

Stories of alcoholics, sexual profligates, drug addicts, liars, thieves, and murderers who have finally admitted their sins, and turned from their evil way, are many and varied. Most likely you know some people who have repented and have been called by their Creator, and turned their lives around to become useful vessels. You may also know of some who did not change, and followed their destructive courses into a literal living hell … and finally were sent to an actual hell, the grave. Loss of hope to recover from addictions of any sort often leads to suicide, insanity, or totally unproductive lives.

We know that even one small sin leads to death, and must be repented of and covered by the atoning sacrifice of Jesus Christ. His shed blood is the only remedy for our stains, the sole formula for remitting sins, and Jesus and the disciples made clear that baptism and the laying on of hands to receive the holy spirit is the route to take from death back to life (Acts 2:38; Matthew 26:28; Mark 1:4; Luke 1:77; 3:3; 24:47; Acts 10:43; Romans 3:25).[4] Without the spirit we are none of His and are dead in our sins (Romans 8:9). There is no other route to the eternal life that we all crave … through the door of His sheepfold (John 10:9).

Herein enters love, for it is a gift of the spirit of God … and the most important amongst faith, hope, and love.

"But the fruit of the spirit is love, joy, peace, longsuffering, kindness, goodness, faithfulness, gentleness, self-control. Against such there is no law" (Galatians 5:22-23).

"And now abide faith, hope, love, these three; but the greatest of these is love" (I Corinthians 13:13).

As we learned earlier, this agape love is "not an impulse from feelings and emotions towards anyone, and does not always follow one's natural inclinations, or gravitate only towards those with whom one finds special affinity."[6] It seeks the welfare of everyone (Romans 15:2). Thus, it is not a feeling that one "works up," though of course it is impossible to separate emotional impacts from rational response; both sides of the brain work together, as we learned in the introduction.[7]

As a fruit of the spirit, we can read Paul's brilliant elucidation of what love is in the love chapter: I Corinthians 13.

"Though I speak with the tongues of men and of angels, but have not love, I have become sounding brass or a clanging cymbal. And though I have the gift of prophecy, and understand all mysteries and all knowledge, and though I have all faith, so that I could remove mountains, but have not love, I am nothing. And though I bestow all my goods to feed the poor, and though I give my body to be burned, but have not love, it profits me nothing. Love suffers long and is kind; love does not envy;

love does not parade itself, is not puffed up; does not behave rudely, does not seek its own, is not provoked, thinks no evil; does not rejoice in iniquity but rejoices in the truth; bears all things, believes all things, hopes all things, endures all things. Love never fails. But whether there are prophecies, they will fail; whether there are tongues, they will cease; whether there is knowledge, it will vanish away" (I Corinthians 13:1-8).

The spirit of Elohim that takes up residence within the person who is called (John 6:44), chosen (Matthew 20:16; 22:14; Revelation 17:14), and repentant (Matthew 3:2; 4:17; Mark 1:15; 6:12; Luke 13:3, 5; Acts 2:38; 17:30; Revelation 2:5, 16, 22; 3:3, 19), is baptized and has hands laid on him (Acts 2:38; 8:17-19; 19:6). This process is summarized in Hebrews 6:1-2. Thence begins a process of growth that the Father guides, to fill the newborn son with

The love of a father for his children is entirely analogous to our heavenly Father's love for us: He feeds, shelters, clothes, and teaches us the ways of living for our eternal joy and prosperity.[8]

more and more of the character of Himself, the same character as the Father wherein love is epitomized (Ephesians 4:13). It is the loving nature found within the Father that inhabits the Son of Man — who is the image of His Father (Colossians 1:15; II Corinthians 3:18; 4:4; I Corinthians 11:7; Romans 8:29) — which image we ourselves will also become in the process of becoming complete (I John 3:2; Philippians 3:21; I Corinthians 15:49; Colossians 3:4; II Peter 1:4).

In love the Father has created us to be like His firstborn Son! This subject is covered in considerable depth in the Fourth Branch. Such truth is emphatically stated in John 17:21-23.

"… that they all may be one as You, Father, are in Me [Jesus Christ], and I in You, that they also may be one in Us, that the world may believe that You have sent Me. And the glory which You gave Me I have given them, that they may be one, even as we are one: I in them, and You in Me, that they may be made perfect in one, and that the world may know that You have sent Me, and have loved them as You have loved Me.."

Love, a fruit of the spirit given to us along with joy, peace, patience, and all the rest — given as a gift along with that spirit, encompassing the law of God that is placed within the called out and chosen sons of God (Hebrews 8:10) — is what envelopes us, what we become as a child of our heavenly Father and a brother of Jesus Christ. Can there be a greater gift than this?

A Lancaster ND 762 flies over the British countryside. A workhorse for the British during World War II, the plane was usually met with a barrage of flak from the German artillery, which sometimes brought down these reliable Allied bombers.[1]

THE THIRD BRANCH

LOVE IS
LAYING DOWN YOUR LIFE

It was May 23, 1944, at one-thirty in the morning when the 22-year-old pilot Ernest Holmes flew his Lancaster ND 762 over the Kempen region of Brabant, with seven other crew on board. His plane was flying back to England after picking out targets in Dortmund. Suddenly Holmes was intercepted by a German fighter plane which opened fire on the Lancaster. "Bail out, bail out!" he shouted when it was clear that the third engine had been hit. Before the crew could jump out there was the sound of a big explosion.

Holmes was slung out of the cockpit but became caught up on the straps of his harness. A sudden turn freed him and he flew through the air. His parachute opened just in time and he landed in the cold grass with only a swollen lip. Four men were killed instantly. He walked across the Landschotse Heath — which ironically was a training ground for German bombers — and had no idea where he was going.

While on her way to milk her father's cows, Netje van der Heijden saw a man in a pilot's uniform and numb from the cold walking in the early morning. She wished him "Good morning," and took him to a safe place, the farmhouse where her parents Fons van der Heijden and Mina van Hoof offered shelter to students in hiding and pilots. Ernest Holmes was neither the first nor the last fugitive for this family. He lodged in a converted chicken shed in the garden, along with two students.

Holmes felt welcome and safe, but he wanted to get back to England as quickly as possible. It soon became clear that this would take longer than expected. He remembered later, emotionally: "A friend of the family begged me, 'Please get away from here. If you are discovered, they will be executed.' Then I realized that they were putting their lives at risk to help me." Holmes finally managed to reach Antwerp with help from Van der Heijden's contacts, where after being betrayed, he ended up in German captivity after all.

Meanwhile the liberation of Netersel was so close that you could almost sense freedom. But on the Wednesday morning of September 20, 1944, German soldiers detained Fons as he was coming out of church. They had found suspicious belongings in his house, so they searched his house again. An injured American soldier who was hiding in the attic of the pig shed was not discovered, but they had sufficient evidence.

Under severe threats to his family, and because he wasn't sure what had been found in his house, Van der Heijden admitted to helping three pilots. In this way he hoped to spare his family and the fugitives who were still there. He was taken to a meadow on the edge of the village, and while he was on his way he saw his oldest brother. "Take care, Sjef, goodbye," he said to him. Then the soldiers shot him in the back and in the head. He died on the spot. In the days that followed the family's farmhouse was completely destroyed: household goods and things of value disappeared; grenades blew holes in the roof and the attic. The six children in the Van der Heijden family fled to Middelbeers; his wife Mina stayed

with her brother. She did not want to leave her husband.

It was only later that Ernest Holmes discovered that the person who had sheltered him had paid for the help he gave others with his life, just before liberation.[2]

Fons van der Heijden gave his life for others in need in the midst of World War II in Holland. He is one of many Dutch and other resisters in various European countries who sheltered Allied soldiers and pilots in the midst of the Nazi holocaust. They literally sacrificed themselves for their friends fighting on the side of good against a military machine bent upon conquering and enslaving all of Europe and England.

How much more, then, can we understand Jesus when he said,

> "Greater love has no one than this, than to lay down one's life for his friends. You are my friends if you do whatever I command you" (John 15:13-14).

"Greater love has no one than this, than to lay down one's life for his friends. You are my friends if you do whatever I command you" (John 15:13-14).

No greater insult and suffering could be applied to an innocent man than a brutal crucifixion ... and not only an innocent person but a sinless One, whose lifeblood was shed for us sinners who are utterly without hope except for this selfless sacrifice for us and for the sins of the whole world... because He loves us.[3]

What an incredible statement that is, to show one's love for another by sacrificing one's own life to save the lives of others, in this case those of the ecclesia, commandment keepers. That is love in the deepest sense.

It is love as shown by the Savior when He chose to die on the stake for each one of us that we might live forever. What an incredible display of love that was, one that made it possible for you and for me to live in the hope each day that our lives are worthwhile because the Son of God thought those lives were valuable enough to die for ... He the Creator of all things visible and invisible (Colossians 1:16)!

Such an expression of love — to die for another — is a tough order to contemplate, since we are so self-centered in our human nature, wanting to preserve the self.

As Paul stated in Romans,

"For when we were yet still without strength, in due time Christ died for the ungodly. For scarcely for a righteous man will one die; yet perhaps for a good man someone would even dare to die. But God demonstrated his own love towards us, in that while we were still sinners, Christ died for us" (Romans 5:6-8).

We as God's ecclesia need to possess the mind of Christ and be willing to die for our brethren should events dictate so … and as prophecies indicate will be the case. In the end time, "Then they will deliver you up to tribulation and kill you, and you will be hated by all nations for My name's sake" (Matthew 24:9). The saints know that death is but a temporary state, a resting in the grave (Job 14:13-15; Daniel 12:2; John 11:11; I Corinthians 15:20, 51; I Thessalonians 4:14), and at the last trumpet, at the resurrection, they will rise with spirit bodies as if in the next moment following their physical death (I Corinthians 15:51-52; I Thessalonians 4:15-17). Physical death is not to be feared, a fear that holds so many in bondage on earth today (Hebrews 2:15), for "death is swallowed up in victory" (I Corinthians 15:54; Isaiah 25:8)! The hope of the resurrection erases the fear of death, when God's love covers over that fear.

Laying down one's life can involve taking time to assist the infirm, those who cannot help themselves. We literally sacrifice our most precious commodity — our time — in giving of ourselves to others.[4]

We sacrifice in other ways besides losing our physical lives through martyrdom. It is clear that our lives dedicated to unveiling the spirit of God within us are "living sacrifices," as it were, as we suppress our selfish nature throughout the day and walk in newness of life through that spirit.

"For Your sake we are killed all day long: we are accounted as sheep for the slaughter" (Psalm 44:22; quoted in Romans 8:36).

"For I through the law died to the law that I might live to God. I have been crucified with Christ; it is no longer I who live, but Christ lives in me, and the life which I now live in the flesh I live by faith in the Son of God, who loved me and gave Himself for me" (Galatians 2:19-20).

"By this we know love, because He laid down His life for us. And we also ought to lay down our lives for the brethren" (I John 3:16).

What is God talking about here? How do we live as being crucified and killed all day long?

Is not this what service to our fellow man is all about? We give of our time and resources and energy to lift up those around us that have need: "And let us not grow weary while doing good …. Therefore, as we have opportunity let us do good to all, especially to those who are of the household of faith" (Galatians 6:9-10). Our human nature wants to serve and aggrandize the self; yet, "Pure and undefiled religion before God and the Father is this: to visit orphans and widows in their trouble, and to keep oneself unspotted from the world" (James 1:27).

We are also told in Matthew 25 to be as the sheep on the right hand of God. The case is made plain for all of us: you serve God by serving others.

"Then the King will say to those on His right hand, 'Come, you blessed of My Father, inherit the kingdom prepared for you from the foundation of the world: for I was hungry and you gave Me food; I was thirsty and you gave Me drink; I was a stranger and you took Me in; I was naked and you clothed Me; I was sick and you visited Me; I was in prison and you came to Me.' Then the righteous will answer Him, saying, 'Lord, when did we see You hungry and feed *You*, or thirsty and give *You* drink? When did we see *You* a stranger and take *You* in, or naked and clothe *You*? Or when did we see You sick, or in prison, and come to You?' And the King will answer and say to them, 'Assuredly, I say to you, inasmuch as you did it to one of the least of these My brethren, you did *it* to Me'" (Matthew 25:34-40).

Isaiah carries the issue even further.

"Wash yourselves, make yourselves clean; put away the evil of your doings from before My eyes. Cease to do evil, learn to do good; seek justice, rebuke the oppressor;

A Pharisee, most zealous in attempting to fulfill the laws of God, along with many manmade laws heaped on top of those, has lost sight of the true meaning of the Law in the first place: to give aid to others in need, doing to others as you would have others to do unto you … which is the entire meaning of the Law and the Prophets.[5]

the widows or fatherless children (Exodus 22: 21-22), but "… do justly, love mercy, and walk humbly with your God" (Micah 6 8). As Jesus warned the scribes and Pharisees, do not neglect the "… weightier matters of the law: justice and mercy and faith" (Matthew 23:23).

Here are some solid ways by which the Eternal shows us how to love by giving of ourselves.

1. Esteem others better than yourself. This is the attitude of Jesus when He washed the disciples' feet on the Passover before He was betrayed (John 13). Though He was Teacher and Lord, He nonetheless placed Himself *beneath* the disciples in terms of how the world looks at government and authority. Think of that: Jesus places Himself "beneath" you, so to speak, in order that He might show what love really is.

Paul reiterated this attitude that Jesus displayed the night He was betrayed when he wrote,

"… fulfill my joy by being like minded, having the same love, being of one accord, of one mind. Let nothing be done through

defend the fatherless, plead for the widow" (Isaiah 1:16-17).

Paul in Romans admonishes us to "Let love be without hypocrisy. Abhor what is evil. Cling to what is good. Be kindly affectionate one to another with brotherly love, in honor giving preference to one another" (Romans 12:9-10). We are not to mistreat or oppress strangers, nor afflict selfish ambition or conceit, but in lowliness of mind let each esteem others better than himself. Let each of you look out not only for his own interests, but also for the interests of others. Let this mind be in you which was also in Christ Jesus ..." (Philippians 2:2-5; see also Ephesians 5:21; Romans 12:10; I Peter 5:5).

Paul continued in the next verses of Philippians to describe how Christ considered Himself *equal* [Greek *isos*, "similar in amount and kind"][6] with the Father, making of himself no reputation and coming as a bond servant, humbling Himself to the point of death ... which merited His being exalted above every name to whom all knees will bow and every tongue will confess.

By esteeming others better than ourselves we place ourselves in a position of being ready to help others with their needs. Pride is suppressed, and we see ourselves as able to do unto others as we would like done to ourselves.

2. Give without expecting anything in return. This is a true attitude of selflessness, for one's actions and time benefit the other person, not oneself. Such selfless giving is a powerful display of love to anyone in need, and was clearly championed by Jesus.

"Give to everyone who asks of you. And from him who takes away your goods do not ask

them back .... But love your enemies, do good, and lend, hoping for nothing in return; and your reward will be great, and you will be sons of the Most High. For He is kind to the unthankful and evil" (Luke 6:30, 35).

Jesus went on to say that you can be confident that, once you give out of a pure heart, expecting nothing in return, you will receive great returns — perhaps things you have never imagined — "... given to you, good measure, pressed down, shaken together, and running over .... For with the same measure that you use, it will be measured back to you" (Luke 6:38).

This is not to say you should expect anything in return ... just that God says you will be rewarded. Those rewards can take many forms: unexpected physical blessings, renewed friendships, or simply the joy of a clean heart in having loved your brother and helped him through a tough spot. David in Psalm 37:26 made it plain that the righteous person is "... ever merciful and lends, and his seed is blessed." Indeed, the Torah admonished a person to relieve another person who has fallen on hard times, even if he is a foreigner or traveler (Leviticus 25:35).

3. Forgive even when it hurts, and love those that hate you. It is hardest of all to forgive someone who has wronged you, but what better way is there to show the love of the Creator, as Jesus so eloquently stated in Matthew 5:39-47:

"But I tell you not to resist an evil person. But whoever slaps you on your right cheek, turn the other to him also. If anyone wants to sue you and take away your tunic, let him have your cloak also. And whoever compels you to go one mile, go with him two. Give to him who asks you and from him who wants to borrow from you do not turn away.

Total forgiveness involves not just an emotional release of the guilt attached to the infraction, but a rational decision to put the problem out of your mind, even as our heavenly Father has removed our shortcomings, upon repentance, as far as the east is from the west.[7]

You have heard that it was said, 'You shall love your neighbor and hate your enemy.' But I say to you, love your enemies, bless those who curse you, do good to those who hate you, and pray for those who spitefully use you and persecute you, that you may be sons of your Father in heaven; for He makes His sun rise on the evil and on the good, and sends rain on the just and on the unjust. For if you love those who love you, what reward have you? Do not even the tax collectors do the same? And if you greet your brethren only, what do you do more than others? Do not even the tax collectors do so?"

By acting beneficently towards one's enemies, a person is reaching towards *perfection* [*teleios*, "complete in mental and moral character"],[8] which is the objective of our walk. By doing good to one's enemies, a person is showing the love that Jesus had even for those who crucified Him, when He said, "Father, forgive them, for they know not what they do" (Luke 23:34). We are to repay no one evil for evil, and are not to avenge ourselves, but rather let the Creator mete out any wrath," ... for vengeance is Mine, I will repay" (Romans 12:19).

> "Therefore if your enemy is hungry, feed him; if he is thirsty, give him a drink; for in so doing you will heap coals of fire on his head. Do not be overcome by evil, but overcome evil with good" (Romans 12:20-21; Proverbs 25:21-22).

Giving of your time and energy even to an enemy is indeed laying down your life for another. If the person with whom there is a conflict will not ask forgiveness from you, then do as Christ did and ask your Father to forgive him (Luke 23:34).

4. Make it a point to reach out to others in need, which is true, undefiled religion (James 1:27). Those in need can be your family, friends, widows, orphaned children, hungry homeless people, or even those who aren't so friendly.

Serving others who cannot help in return changes one's perspectives on life, opening doors of hope and joy, not only to the person being helped but to yourself as well.

Giving of yourself to others in their need is our calling to love. Jesus allowed Himself to be sacrificed on the stake because He knew the need for all of mankind to be forgiven of their sins — the perfect for the imperfect. So likewise we must sacrifice of ourselves, if not literally by giving up our lives if necessary, then by sacrificing our time and energy for those suffering and in need. Pure, undefiled love is to lay down your life for your friends (John 15:13).

DO YOU KNOW WHAT I HAVE DONE TO YOU?

THE FOURTH BRANCH

LOVE IS GOD MULTIPLYING HIMSELF

Why did God choose to create mankind? He could have just continued on with His eternal existence and left things as they were … but He did not, nor could He! It is the inherent nature of our great Father in heaven to multiply, to grow, to enlarge Himself as a manifestation of His love.

How do we know this?

1. God tells us this is His nature: "Of the *increase* [*marbeh*, "increasing"][1] of His government and peace there will be no end" (Isaiah 9:7). To increase His government endlessly there must be a continually increase

The bliss in living within the Garden of Eden — the Paradise of God — is the environment within which the Creator intended all of us to experience and enjoy every day. It seems that all aspects of this present world are designed to rob that Edenic bliss from us, and replace love with hatred and division. Yet, Eden will ultimately return and replace the present-day thralldom to decay.[2]

of individuals to administer that government. We are also, on a spiritual plane, admonished to continually grow in truth, love, grace, and knowledge of Jesus Christ (Ephesians 4:15; I Peter 2:2; II Peter 3:16).

2. All of created life has as its passion the built-in desire to increase, to multiply, as was God's command to living creatures (Genesis 1:20), birds (Genesis 1:22), mankind (Genesis 1:28; 9:1), and by extension to all living organisms, from single-celled microbes to the huge whales. Biology has shown that reproduction after its kind is essential for the survival of all species … especially after mankind sinned and was removed from the Garden of Eden: "I will greatly multiply your sorrow and your conception" (Genesis 3:16), and not just for people, but for all of the creation, for death dogged the lives of all creatures as the perfect environment deteriorated from its perfection.

So, "God created man in His own image; in the *image* of God He created him: male and female He created them" (Genesis 1:27). Man was created in the likeness of God (Genesis 5:1; 9:6), and in fact Adam was a son of God, as the lineage of Christ is outlined in Luke 3; see verse 38.

Yet, the similitude of this new creation to the Creator Himself cannot be minimized. The word image in Hebrew is *tselem*,[3] and in context in Genesis 1:27 it means "replica," of the same essential nature, like Adam begetting Seth "after his image [*tselem*]," who was the "spitting image" of the father, as we might say, or something very close to it, with fingers, eyes, arms, legs, internal organs, and a nature just like the original.

What greater love could our Father in heaven reveal than to reproduce Himself in multiple billions of individuals throughout the 6,000 years of mankind's history on earth? He emptied Himself of being the only One, along with Jesus Christ and other sons of Elohim and angels (Hebrews 1), to exist. From one man — Adam — He has made billions of individuals in His image, each with the potential to become God, a part of the family of Elohim (I John 3:2; Psalm 82:6; John 10:33-38; Romans 8:29) — if we believe what Jesus has said in His word:

"For whom He foreknew he also predestined to be conformed to the image of His Son, that He might be the firstborn among many brethren" (Romans 8:29).

"Beloved, now we are children of God and it has not yet been revealed what we shall be, but we know that when He is revealed, we shall be like Him, for we shall see Him as He is" (I John 3:2).

We understand that reproduction of a kind occurs in the physical realm — God needed to divide Adam into male and female for procreation to occur (Genesis 2:20-24; 1:28) — but after being resurrected, humans will not reproduce (Matthew 22:30; Mark 12:25), like the spirit messengers in heaven do not reproduce. Spirit beings apparently possess both sexes in one super being, like Adam did before Eve — the female essence — was separated from him. Before that separation he was a son of Elohim, possessing both sexes (Luke 3:38).

So … how can we be sure that we, the saints, will become just like Jesus Christ, apart from the direct assurances already stated? Let us take a look at the identities of Jesus Christ and the elect that are revealed in Scripture, for they are many.

1. WE HAVE AN ETERNAL NATURE. — PAST ETERNAL EXISTENCE —
Jesus Christ

He was with the Father (a spirit), in heaven before becoming flesh and blood.

"In the beginning was the Word, and the Word was with God, and the Word was God.

He was in the beginning with God. All things were made through Him, and without Him nothing was made that was made.... And the Word became flesh and dwelt among us ..." (John 1:1-3, 14).

"No one has ascended to heaven but He who came down from heaven, that is, the Son of Man who is in heaven" (John 3:13). *Heaven* (Strong 3772) = *ouranos*, "the sky (elevated in height); by extension, heaven (as the abode of God)."[4]

"He who believes in Me, believes not in Me but in Him who sent Me [the Father in heaven, where Christ was also].... For I have not spoken on My own authority; but the Father who sent Me gave Me a command ..." (John 12:44, 49).

"And now, Father, glorify Me together with Yourself, with the glory which I had with You before the world was" (John 17:5).

The Elect

The idea that the elect existed in spirit form before being born as flesh and blood, like Jesus Christ was, may surprise you, and frankly you may reject the idea. I personally believe that the Scriptures teach that we did exist before being conceived and born on earth, but such an idea is not essential for salvation. You can accept or reject the idea, but here are words of God to consider.

"Then the dust will return to the earth as it was, and the spirit will return to God who gave it" (Ecclesiastes 12:7). Thus, the spirit, the "real person", was once with God who is in heaven.

"And again: 'Here am I [Yahweh = Jesus Christ] and the children [the elect] whom the Lord [the Father] has given Me [Jesus Christ; quoted from Isaiah 8:18]. *Inasmuch then as the children [the elect] have partaken of flesh and blood, He Himself* [Jesus Christ] *likewise shared in the same,* that through death He might destroy him who had the power of death, that is, the devil ..." (Hebrews 2:13-14; emphasis mine).

Just as Jesus Christ became flesh and blood, but before was a spirit, so the elect were first eternal spirit with God before they became flesh and blood. The analogy between Christ's and the elect's state is unmistakable. Adam, from whom all of mankind has descended (Acts 17:26), came directly as a "spirit germ" or template from God's express image (Genesis 1:26-27, 2:7), a son of God (Luke 3:38). The elect, physically speaking, have come from Adam through generations of procreation, carrying his genes ... which are exact copies of God's spiritual form (now converted to physical).

This fact explains why God could know beforehand — before converting the spirits of Elohim into flesh and blood — those who were predestined to be conformed to the image of Jesus Christ, walking in His footsteps and inheriting salvation. To predestine them He had to know them beforehand. This explains why He could call them "brethren", and how he "knew" them, for they were of His same spiritual genetic family, sons of God [Elohim] in heaven before becoming flesh.

"For whom He foreknew [before being made flesh and blood, as spirits in the spirit world], He also predestined to be conformed to the image of His Son, that He might be the firstborn among many brethren. Moreover whom He predestined, these He also called; whom He called, these He also justified, and whom He justified, these He also glorified" (Romans 8:29-30).

"Blessed be the God and Father of our Lord Jesus Christ, who has blessed us with every spiritual blessing in the heavenly places in Christ, just as He [the Father] chose us in Him [Christ] before the foundation of the world, that we should be holy and without blame before Him in love, having predestined us to adoption as sons by Jesus Christ to Himself, according to the good pleasure of His will... that in the dispensation of the fullness of the times He might gather together in one all things in Christ, both which are in heaven and which are on earth — in Him. In Him

also we have obtained an inheritance, being predestined according to the purpose of Him ..." (Ephesians 1:3-5, 10-11).

— FLESHLY EXISTENCE ON EARTH —

Jesus Christ

Jesus Christ came to earth as flesh and blood. "And the Word became flesh and dwelt among us" (John 1:14).

"For what the law could not do in that it was weak through the flesh, God did by sending His own Son in the likeness

Jesus Christ — the Word — left His royal estate in heaven and came to earth to preach His Father's message of abundant life to all who would hear Him. That message resounds just as strongly today as it did two millennia ago.[5]

of sinful flesh, on account of sin: He condemned sin in the flesh ..." (Romans 8:3).

The Elect

Man is a "nephesh" on earth, a "living soul" as stated in Genesis 2:7. Possessing the human spirit that imparted intellect and gave him form and being in God's image, man reflected the human life in the material world that continued the motile power under control of the spirit reality, which he is.

Nephesh (Strong 5315) = "a breathing creature, i.e. animal or (abstract) vitality."[6]

"Inasmuch then as the children [the elect] have partaken of flesh and blood ..." (Hebrews 2:14).

Our physical creation is through the spirit of man in coordination with (perhaps part and parcel with) the egg and sperm, which gives rise to the physical being; see Psalm 139:13-16:

"For You have formed my inward parts;
You have covered me in my mother's womb.
I will praise You, for I am fearfully and
   wonderfully made;
Marvelous are Your works,
And that my soul knows very well.
My frame was not hidden from You,
When I was made in secret,
And skillfully wrought in the lowest parts
   of the earth.

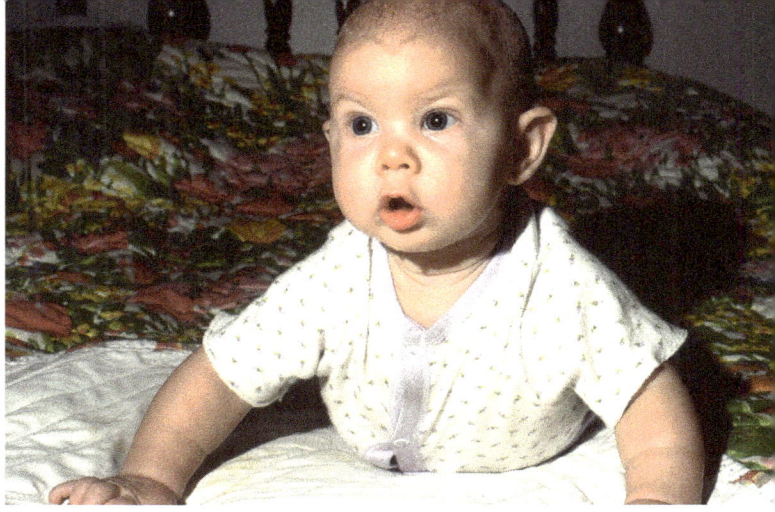

We humans are created in the express image of the heavenly Father, and like Jesus live on this earth for but a short time, being given the choice to either obey or reject Him. Those that rceive His calling and receive His spirit will reign with Christ for a thousand years.[7]

Your eyes saw my substance, being yet
   unformed.
And in Your book they all were written,
The days fashioned for me,
When as yet there were none of them."

— FUTURE ETERNAL EXISTENCE—

Jesus Christ

"And now, O Father, glorify Me together with Yourself, with the glory which I had with You before the world was" (John 17:5).

Jesus Christ is now at the right hand of God the Father in heaven, to live eternally with Him (Acts 2:33-34; 5:31; 7:55-56; Ephesians 1:20; Colossians 3:1; Hebrews 1:3, 13; 8:1; 10:12; 12:2; I Peter 3:22).

"Then the seventh angel sounded: And there were loud voices in heaven, saying, 'The kingdoms of this world have become the kingdoms of our Lord and of His Christ, and He shall reign forever and ever!'" (Revelation 11:15).

The Elect

"And there shall be no more curse, but the throne of God and the Lamb shall be in it, and His servants shall serve Him.... And they shall reign forever and ever" (Revelation 22:3, 5).

"To him who overcomes I will grant to sit with Me on My throne, as I also overcame and sat down with My Father on His throne" (Revelation 3:21).

"Behold, I tell you a mystery: We shall not all sleep, but we shall all be changed — in a moment, in the twinkling of an eye, at the last trumpet. For the trumpet will sound, and the dead will be raised incorruptible …" (I Corinthians 15:51-52).

"For the Lord Himself will descend from heaven with a shout, with a voice of an archangel, and with the trumpet of God. And the dead in Christ will rise first. Then we who are alive and remain shall be caught up together with them in the clouds to meet the Lord in the air. And thus we shall always be with the Lord" (I Thessalonians 4:16-17).

For details on the remaining 24 identities of the saints with Christ, please refer to the end notes for supporting scriptural evidence.

2. WE ARE DESTINED TO RECEIVE RULERSHIP OVER THE NATIONS AS SPIRITS.[8]

3. WE ARE TO INHERIT ALL THINGS.[9]

Even as Jesus was raised to eternal life, so the saints will be raised, at the last trumpet, when He returns to reign with the saints for a thousand years.[8]

4. WE RECEIVE GOD'S SPIRIT BY BAPTISM AND THE LAYING ON OF HANDS.[11]

5. WE ARE SPIRITUAL BROTHERS, WITH THE SAME FATHER, FAMILY, AND POTENTIAL.[12]

6. WE ARE SENT TO EARTH BY THE FATHER.[13]

7. WE WILL REIGN WITH THE FATHER ON HIS THRONE.[14]

8. WE WILL BE WORSHIPED [ONLY GODS CAN BE WORSHIPED].[15]

9. WE PRAY DIRECTLY TO THE FATHER.[16]

10. THE FATHER SPEAKS DIRECTLY TO US.[17]

11. WE ENDURE TRIALS, SUFFER, AND OVERCOME AS LIVING SACRIFICES.[18]

12. WE ARE MINISTERED TO BY ANGELS.[19]

13. WE FORGIVE THE SINS OF OTHERS.[20]

14. CHRIST AND THE ELECT ARE EQUIVALENT AT THE RESURRECTION.[21]

15. THE LAW IS WRITTEN IN OUR HEARTS, WE DO THE FATHER'S WILL, AND WE HAVE HIS MIND.[22]

16. WE ARE GIVEN A NAME THAT NO ONE ELSE KNOWS.[23]

17. WE ARE TO BE EXAMPLES OF GODLY LIVING TO THE WORLD.[24]

Even as our Savior prayed to the Father continually, so we as His servants must pray without ceasing to our heavenly Father, who answers in every case, though not always in the way we might expect.[9]

18. **THERE IS HOPE OF GREAT GLORY IN THE SPIRIT REALM AFTER PHYSICAL DEATH.**[25]

19. **WE HAVE BEEN SENT INTO THE WORLD.**[26]

20. **WE ARE NOT OF THE WORLD.**[27]

21. **WE ARE TEMPTED WITH EVIL**[28]

22. **WE WERE ORDAINED BEFORE THE FOUNDATION OF THE WORLD TO BE SONS OF GOD.**[29]

23. **WE WERE MADE A LITTLE LOWER THAN THE ANGELS.**[30]

24. **WE WILL BE RAISED BY THE SPIRIT OF THE FATHER IN US.**[31]

25. **WE ARE JOINT HEIRS OF SALVATION.**[32]

What a magnificent rendition of the truth that **we, as called and chosen disciples of Jesus Christ, over time become more and more like our Savior ... transformed into His very image!** We reflect the Eternal's glory like mirrors! This is referring in part to our becoming like Him in character as we put down the pulls of the flesh and live by His spirit (Galatians 5:22-24), but the ultimate conclusion of the matter is to become very God in spirit conformation at the resurrection, even as we now are made in His image while fleshly beings (Genesis 1:26-27; I Corinthians 15:42-54; I John 3:2): "... when He shall appear, we shall be like Him ...", and when you have seen Christ [who looked like us] you know what the Father looks like in the spirit realm: see John 14:9.

The "walk" that Jesus Christ and the saints experience is the same, differing only in terms of specifics relevant to the age in which one lives. We follow Christ's example, walking in His footsteps (I John 2:26; I Peter 2:21) Just

Though our exuberant lifestyle in the heavenly realm can only be faintly understood by us humans in this physical realm, it will be infinitely more rewarding and joyous than we can possibly imagine.[24]

as Jesus would do only the will of the Father (Luke 1:49; John 5:19), so the brethren are to do the exclusive will of the Father (Matthew 6:10; Mark 3:35). The only difference between Jesus and us is that He was directly born of the Father and sinless, while we are indirectly born of the Father — through Adam — and have sinned ... though we are now washed clean by His perfect sacrifice!

Not only that, but the saints have God's spirit to know all things, just like Jesus Christ has all knowledge because of His intimate contact with the Father.

"But as it is written, 'Eye has not seen, nor ear heard, neither has entered into the heart of man the things which God has prepared for them that love Him.' But God has revealed them unto us by His spirit: for the spirit searches all things, yes, the deep things of God. For what man knows the things of a man, save the spirit of man which is in him? Even so the things of God knows no man, but the spirit of God" (I Corinthians 2:9-11).

In Conclusion ...

The preexistence of Jesus Christ as one of Elohim, His life on earth as a human being, and His eternal life in heaven, are a picture of each one of the elect of the Father. We are born, live, suffer, and die, and finally will be raised from the dead as was Christ. Recall that Jesus Christ ". . came unto His own ..." (*unto His own = idios*, "one's own, by implication private or

separate"),[33] and although these predestined people of Israel for the most part did not recognize Immanuel when He came, yet "... as many as received Him, to them He gave power [the right or privilege] to become the Sons of God" (John 1:11-12). The others of Israel who rejected Him the first time will surely be given the opportunity to accept Him as Messiah once the veil of disbelief is lifted from their understanding. They will be a part of the second resurrection, for God has declared that all of Israel shall be saved (Romans 11:26; Jeremiah 3:18).

There are differences between Christ and the elect, of course, in that the preexisting Spirit from which each one is derived is unique. Even the weak among the elect are to be granted eternal, scintillatingly rewarding and stupendous positions in the Kingdom after the resurrection.

"In My Father's house [the heavenly Zion] are many *mansions* [Greek *mone*, "residences and responsibilities"];[34] if it were not so, I would have told you. I go to prepare a place for you" (John 14:2).

"And behold, I am coming quickly, and My reward is with Me, to give to every one according to his *work*" [Greek *ergon*, or the effort or occupation he will enjoy in the Kingdom] (Revelation 22:12).

Those positions are already allotted for

the elect; see I Corinthians 12:18:

> "But now God has set the members, each one of them, in the body just as He pleased."

To realize that one's eternal future holds joys, fulfillment, position, glory, and accomplishment no less vivid than those of Jesus Christ is a most astounding realization. Since the increase of God's government is endless (Isaiah 9:7), it is highly likely that planets in far flung galaxies will become inhabited by God's saints and new creations. This is the type of future that our Father has promised for each of His creatures … and He will do it out of love.

The family model about which humankind — and most of the animal and plant world — revolve is placed here for no small reason. The family pictures the very progression of man from conception, to gestation, to birth, to growth to adulthood — progressing from being a son (or daughter) to becoming a father or mother. This progression continues through generations, increasing the number of those who can be raised as sons of God, increasing the government

of God endlessly … or at least as long as reproduction and families continue. Recall that God said through Paul that "The invisible things of Him from the creation of the world are clearly seen, being understood by the things that are made, even His

Like the spiral formation of sunflower seeds in the head, or the spiraling galaxies of the universe — governed by the "golden mean" — so will the increase of God's government continue to multiply without limit to occupy every corner of space.[35]

eternal power and Godhead, so that they are without excuse" (Romans 1:20).

What incredible love towards us our Creator has shown to have us to be His sons, alongside Jesus Christ at His throne.

That is love expressed in its deepest sense.

As Elohim multiplies Himself, God's selfless love reveals that just as He is the I AM (Exodus 3:14), so will we become self-existent ones who will live forever. Satan hates that truth, and makes plain why he

> "Since the increase of God's government is endless (Isaiah 9:7), it is highly likely that planets in far flung galaxies will become inhabited by God's saints and new creations.

has so besmirched and dirtied the beauty and purpose of sex — to reproduce more people in God's image — and has caused the erosion of family values so essential for the upbringing of Godly people. This adversary has so corrupted the moral judgment of many leaders in education and government that they claim a person can somehow change his or her sex by merely

making such a claim. Homosexuality, transgenderism, and all other sorts of perversions are promoted as being good and acceptable ... the end result being that fewer potential sons of God will be born, and therefore fewer replacements there will be for Satan who, in his own demented thinking, believes that somehow he can even yet thwart God's plan and be placed upon the throne of the earth forever ... even as he now is the god of this world (II Corinthians 4:4; Ephesians 2:2). Yet, his doom is sure: being thrown into the abyss for 1,000 years during the millennium (Revelation 10:1-3) and, after being released following that Eden on earth, burned up in the lake of fire for permanent destruction (Revelation 20:10).

God's love is so expansive that He is multiplying Himself, and will hand us an eternity of joy and peace beyond anything we can imagine. That is the humility of the God who made us.

The Ancient of Days

Right
(Righteousness)
Obedience to Law
Light

Satan the Devil

Wrong
(Unrighteousness)
Disobedience to Law
Darkness

2 Forms of Government on Earth
from Liberty to Totalitarianism

• God's Government
within the ecclesia

• Satan's Government
within the world

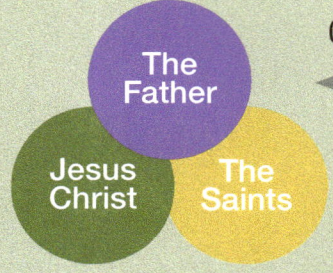

Gradations between

Satan
Highest officials
Mid-level officials
Low-level officials
The masses

- **The spirit of brotherhood, or each looking upon others as better than oneself**
(Matthew 20:25-28; Luke 22:24-27; John 13:2-15; 17:20-23; Romans 8:29; 12:10; Philippians 2:1-5; Ephesians 5:21; I Peter 5:5)

- **Each is equally valuable, with "the least being the greatest"**
(Luke 9:48; Matthew 23:11-12)

- **Service to others with one's spiritual gifts, given at baptism and the laying on of hands, is one's essential duty**
(I Corinthians 12; Romans 12:6-8; I Peter 4:10)

- **A spirit of love and forgiveness**
(II Timothy 1:7; Galatians 5:22-23; John 13:34; 15:12, 17; Romans 12:10; 13:8; Ephesians 4:2; Luke 17:3-4; Matthew 18:21-22)

- **The spirit of domination over others, looking upon others as more inferior down the pyramidal structure**
(Matthew 20:25; Luke 22:24-25)

- **Value depends on position within the pyramid, with "the highest being the greatest"** [1]
(Luke 22:25; *lordship = kyrieuo*, "to exercise control over: and *authority over = exousiazo*, "to exercise power or authority over anyone"; Mark 10:42; *lordship = katakurieuo*, "to control, subjugate; *authority = katexousiazo*, "to wield full privilege over")

- **Control over others to order them as slaves**
(see the references above)

- **A spirit of self-centeredness and narcissism**
(II Timothy 3:1-5; Romans 1:28-31; Galatians 5:19-21)

THE FIFTH BRANCH

LOVE IS
LIVING HIS GOVERNMENT

The love of God is pictured beautifully through the elect living in harmony with one another, serving one another with their gifts. The government of Elohim allows this love to flow freely, while the government of Satan brings one into captivity to others. So, we see the eternal conflict between obedience to God and obedience to that which is not of God.

The changes in government throughout Biblical history are most interesting to explore. One first notes a perfectly harmonious government in Eden, based on perfect love, with Adam and Eve living within a perfect environment designed to optimize mankind's joy and health of body, mind, and spirit. Their contact was directly with the Creator, whom they obeyed without questioning.

With disobedience due to the Adversary's temptation, Adam and Eve were expelled from the Garden of Eden and began a life outside the Garden.[2] They procreated

children, many, many of them, as did their children, grandchildren, and subsequent generations up to the Great Flood. It was a time of disarray and conflict — their thoughts were evil continually (Genesis 6:11-13) — but before all flesh were killed in the Flood there were at least 10 billion people on earth, possibly many more.[3] Satan could not prevent the multiplication of humankind, each one a potential son of Elohim. The Adversary could not stop this marvelous plan of procreation of mankind in His own image that would ultimately replace Satan on the throne of a new world.

That replacement would require a resurrection of these beings made in God's image (Revelation 20:12-13), which would have to wait for several millennia.

Meanwhile, the Flood arrived and wiped out all but eight people[4] — Noah's family — who after the Flood began multiplying once again, as commanded by the Creator (Genesis 9:1). The plan of Elohim to overspread the earth with His families was temporarily interrupted by Nimrod, the grandson of Ham (Genesis 10:6-8), at Babel, when he convinced the 70 families of nations to congregate around Babel and other cities which were constructed through the evil plans of this arch-enemy of God.[5] He built Babel, Erech, Accad, and Calneh, and Asshur, and constructed a tower, a symbol of unity for all peoples to organize a society suppressing the Eternal's plans (Genesis 10:9; 11:1-9).

Even after cleansing the earth of its sinful population, it did not take long for tyranny to once again raise its ugly head as Nimrod and his compatriots built a tower at Babel, a symbol of worship of human leaders to try and prevent the families from migrating to their designated places across the earth.[7]

"And the Lord said, 'Behold, the people are one, and they have all one language, and this they begin to do; and now nothing will be restrained from them which they have imagined to do'" (Genesis 11:6).

Thus, the Eternal confounded the languages of the various families and caused them to migrate (scatter) to their appointed lands across the earth.[8] Then the tribes of mankind multiplied as Noah had been commanded. Out of this focus of civilization at Sumer came Abram, a man who, according to the Book of Jasher, was the son of a servant of Nimrod

Mankind multiplied mightily before the Great Flood, but so did tyranny and evil, such that Elohim had to wipe out all of the evil people except for eight souls. Sheer numbers of people does not guarantee righteousness in their living.[6]

himself.[9] Abram grew up directly in the shadow and teaching of Shem, and was recognized by the Eternal as a man of great faith and loyalty to the laws of God. He was appointed as the one to begin the process of redeeming mankind from the sure result of sin and rebellion to the Creator … which is death, eternal, unplaced death and annihilation unless atoned for by a perfect sacrifice. That sacrifice was to be Jesus Christ, the Lion of the tribe of Judah, who would come from Abram's descendants many generations later.

Then began the trek out of sin, as it were, as Abram was given the great commissions of race and grace … to journey to the land of Canaan, not knowing where he was going but going because he believed God when He spoke.[10] Ultimately he had a son of promise — Isaac — who in turn bore Jacob, whose 12 sons ended up in Goshen in Egypt at the behest of Joseph, the son sold into slavery by his jealous brothers.[11] Israel grew greatly within Egypt, and escaped the harsh hand of Pharaoh through the Red Sea, wandered 40 years in the Wilderness of Sinai, and finally entered Canaan to set up the nation of Israel.[12]

The nation split into the Northern Kingdom, called Israel, and the Southern Kingdom called Judah, both of which were eventually taken captive due to their sins and shipped to the outlying lands of their captors, Assyria and Babylon.[14] There the people prospered for many years, and many eventually migrated north and west to inhabit portions of northern and western Europe, Scandinavia, and the British Isles. The people flourished as they went, and in due time began to spill over into the Americas, parts of Africa, Australia, New Zealand, and other parts of the world.[15]

In the meantime, a contingent of the descendants of Judah returned to Jerusalem after 70 years in captivity.[16] This return made

Abraham, the father of the faithful, was selected by the Creator to begin the process of reclaiming mankind from the sure death that results from sin. He journeyed wherever he was told to go, obeyed the laws and statutes of God, and as a result was promised incredible rewards of descendants and land.[13]

possible the birth of the Messiah through Joseph and Mary, the Eternal procreating His own Son as the Savior of all mankind, the One who lived a sinless life and was brutally crucified at the hands of depraved men. Yet, according to the Father's plan He was raised on the third day and ascended to the Father's throne,[17] and shortly thereafter the New Covenant ecclesia was established.[18] That ecclesia spread throughout the world to all nations, now that the spirit of God was extended to gentile nations.

Mankind continued to multiply in all nations over the face of the earth as history moved on through the Dark Ages, Middle Ages, and on into the Modern Era. Wars and calamities continued periodically, but the population of men made in God's image multiplied, such that by the beginning of the 21st Century about 7 billion people graced the earth … possibly approaching as many inhabitants of earth as before the Flood. Through these centuries following Christ's brief life on earth, the ecclesia was persecuted by governments and false religious organizations that attempted to wipe out the truths that had been revealed through the Son of Man. Yet, the word of God and the true ecclesia could not be wiped out, even though attempts were made to nullify its messages by corrupt organizations like the Roman Catholic Church, which proclaimed that it was the true, universal church. The true ecclesia was always small,[19] but always potent.

Yet, even the Popes, governments, and leaders in education throughout the world could not wipe out the truth that Jesus Christ will return a second time and establish His rulership over the earth. That truth in His word could not be obliterated — only suppressed — the truth that Eden would be restored to fill the entire earth, not just a garden in the Middle East. That truth, and the mystery hidden from ages and generations[20] that the saints will inherit kingship in a new age, and reestablish the true understanding of love and joy to all the world, was begun through one man — Abraham — and will be expanded to include all people made in God's image, that have for now been blinded to the truth.

Throughout the annals of history, since Adam and Eve were thrust out of the Garden of Eden until today, there have been many sorts of government, ranging from totalitarianism to total liberation. Only within the Garden of Eden was there unbridled liberty and freedom of oppression of men by other men[21]; that freedom will be renewed in the wonderful world to come, the millennial reign of Jesus Christ on earth. Pure liberty can only be achieved by a people free of sin, willfully obeying the Creator so there is no need of policing power to protect people from predation and injury by others. That is the beauty of Eden's government: total submission to the One that created mankind in His own image.

The governments of men can take many forms, and have been categorized in different ways. One classification arrives at 16 types of government, as outlined below.[22]

Totalitarian rulers have done incredible damage to the innate quality of people created to be free before their Creator and live in peace with their fellow man, typified by Fidel Castro of Cuba (lower right), Idi Amin of Uganda (upper left), Joseph Stalin of Russia (upper right), and Adolph Hitler of Germany (lower left).[23]

1. Republic. A government whose authority is based on citizen's votes which are represented by elected or nominated officials chosen in free elections.

2. Democracy. Democracy means "rule of the people". The term today refers to a political system in which the people or their elected representatives govern themselves.

3. Theocracy. A government where priests rule in the name of God or by officials who are regarded as divinely guided, or consistent with the principles of a particular religion.

4. Autocracy. A government controlled by absolute power, and in the hands of a single person with minimal restraints on any decisions, and lack of any mechanism of popular control.

5. Technocracy. A government where scientists and technical experts are in control of the state, and where rulers are selected on the basis of their knowledge or skill rather than their wealth or power.

6. Fascism. A way of ruling that advocates total control of the people, and seeks to promote ancestral and cultural values and eradicate foreign influences. It involves government controlling business through regulations.

7. Anarchy. A state with the absence of law, wherein abides lawlessness and disorder, usually resulting from a failure of government.

8. Monarchy. A government where supreme authority is vested in a single and usually hereditary figure, such as a king, and whose powers can vary from absolute to none at all.

9. Oligarchy. Rule of the few, where power effectively rests with a faction of persons or families.

10. Plutocracy. Government rule by the rich or powerful provided by wealth, often used to describe a wealthy class ruling a government, and oftentimes from behind the scenes.

11. Tyranny. The government or authority of an absolute ruler who arbitrarily exercises power over subjects without control by law and justice.

12. Totalitarian. A system in which a single political authority regulates total control over the state, that is centralized and dictatorial.

13. Federation. A political organization characterized by the union of small states, groups, or parties which are self-governed in internal affairs, and are united under a central government.

14. Communism. A system of government in which the state owns and operates industry on behalf of the people, while suppressing religious beliefs and individual initiative.

15. Junta. A group or coalition that takes control of the state after overthrowing a government, usually by a military group.

16. Dictatorship. A form of government where the power rests entirely on one person or a group of persons, which rule can be acquired by inheritance or force, and is usually oppressive.

All of these forms of government assume the rule of men over men, true to the definition of government, "the exercise of authority over a state, district, organization, institution, etc.; a system of ruling or controlling."[24] The history of mankind has known no other way, and the reason is because people have not known how to love their Creator or their fellow man.

We All Must Become Shepherds

To live God's government is to learn to be shepherds. In the process of growing towards the fullness of Christ's and the Father's character (II Peter 3:18) it is critical to do certain things, some of them that have been

We are like sheep, tending to follow the flock of others around us due to peer pressure, so we need a shepherd ... and the One Shepherd that we can totally count on to lead us in the right direction is Jesus Christ.[25]

discussed in other chapters of this book.

1. Utilize the gifts of the spirit that have been granted to you. These gifts are given to each of us as our Father in heaven has desired (I Corinthians 12:18), gifts which are described in all of I Corinthians 12. We are admonished to use these gifts to uplift one another (I Peter 4:10; Romans 12:6-8), for our Father has invested heavily in us to bear fruit from His intervention in our lives.

2. Grow in love — the agape sort — which is summarized in I Corinthians 13:1-8.

"Though I speak with the tongues of men and of angels, but have not love, I have become sounding brass or a clanging cymbal. And though I have the gift of prophecy, and understand all mysteries and all knowledge, and though I have all faith, so that I could remove mountains, but have not love, I am nothing. And though I bestow all my goods to feed the poor, and though I give my body to be burned, but have not love, it profits me nothing. Love suffers long and is kind; love does not envy; love does not parade itself, is not puffed up; does not behave rudely, does not seek its own, is not provoked, thinks no evil; does not rejoice in iniquity, but rejoices in the truth; bears all things, believes all things, hopes all things, endures all things. Love never fails. But whether there are prophecies, they will fail; whether there are tongues, they will cease; whether there is knowledge, it will vanish away."

Without love for one another, the sort that allowed Jesus to bear our sins and willingly die on the stake for each of us, we can never hope to achieve the mind of Him, for such outgoing selflessness is the principle that must utterly consume us. It is the essence of being subject one to another (Ephesians 5:21; Philippians 2:3; I Peter 5:5). Jesus so greatly emphasized the need to love one another as He first loved us, for by this we will be identified as His disciples (John 13:34-35; 15:12). Moreover, "Greater love has no one than to lay down one's life for his friends. You are My friends if you do whatever I command you" (John 15:13-14).

John in I John 3:14-16 states,

"We know that we have passed from death to life, because we love the brethren. He who does not love his brother abides in death. Whoever hates his brother is a murderer, and you know that no murderer has eternal life abiding in him. By this we know love, because He laid down His life for us, and we also ought to lay down our lives for the brethren."

3. Grow in forgiveness. Forgiving others is such an essential part of God's character that Jesus answered Peter's question, "Lord, how often shall my brother sin against me, and I forgive him? Up to seven times?" (Matthew 18:21). Jesus' answer is simple. "I do not say to you, up to seven times, but up to seventy times seven" (Matthew 18:22).

In Luke the situation is made even more clear. "If your brother sins against you, rebuke him, and if he repents, forgive him. And if he sins against you seven times in a day, and seven times in a day returns to you, saying, 'I repent,' you shall forgive him" (Luke 17:3-4).

Forgiveness is to be extended to the person if he realizes he has sinned against you and asks for forgiveness, but if the offender does not ask for forgiveness, then we must ask the Father to forgive them, as Christ did on the stake: "Father, forgive them, for they do not know what they do" (Luke 23:34).

Forgiveness takes away the stress of harboring hatred and grudges towards others, giving health and longer, more fulfilling life. The instructions are simple: "Forgive us of our debts, as we forgive our debtors" (Matthew 6:12), and as Paul said in Romans,

"Repay no one evil for evil. Have regard for good things in the sight of all men. If it is possible, as much as depends on you, live peaceably with all men. Beloved, do not avenge yourselves, but rather give place to wrath, for it is written, 'Vengeance is Mine; I will repay,' says the Lord. Therefore, 'If your enemy is hungry, feed him; if he thirsts, give him a drink, for in so doing you will heap coals of fire on his head'. Do not be overcome by evil, but overcome evil with good" (Romans 12:17-21).

4. Encourage and comfort one another in every place and opportunity you have, to not just hang on to the truth but move forward with it in vigor and hope every day. This point will be reemphasized in the tenth branch of the vine. Note how Paul and Peter encouraged the brethren in many circumstances (Acts 11:23; 16:40; 20:2,; 27:36; Romans 1:12; I Corinthians 14:3; Philippians 2:19; Colossians 2:2; I Thessalonians 3:2). The two Greek words translated *encourage* or *encouraged* are *parakaleo* ("to exhort, admonish, persuade, beseech, implore, encourage, comfort, to be cheered")[25] and *euthumos* ("good cheer or courage, cheerful").[26] Paul also strove to comfort the brethren, as in I Thessalonians 4:18, where he explained events surrounding the resurrection and the fact that the brethren would forever be with Jesus and the Father. Twenty-one verses in Acts through II Thessalonians use the words *parakaleo, paregoria* ("comfort, solace, consolation"), or *paraklesis* ("exhortation, excitement, persuasion, cheering and supporting influence").[27] These verses all show that we need to uplift and persuade our brethren to endure to the end (Matthew 24:13) in the midst of an evil and perverse world, for "... lawlessness will abound and the love of many will grow cold" (Matthew 24:12).

This encouragement of our brethren ought to flow throughout fellowship opportunities, as described in I Corinthians 14. All of the brethren are encouraged to *prophesy* [*propheteuo*],[28] or speak inspired words from one's indwelling spirit, while others *judge* [*diakrino*][29] what is said. By everyone participating in speaking, the opportunities to uplift one's brethren are multiplied compared to having just one person speak in a corporate, programmed type of structure.

5. To be a shepherd of God's people we must indeed follow in the footsteps of Jesus Christ and become shepherds, like Him. Peter called Jesus the Chief Shepherd (I Peter 5:4) ... not the only shepherd but the Chief Shepherd, because He is the "... firstborn of many brethren ..." (Romans 8:29). He is the One prophesied to "...shepherd My people Israel" (Matthew 2:6). As the elect, we understand that after

the resurrection we will be ruling as Kings and Priests on the earth, teaching survivors of the Great Tribulation the wonderful ways of the Creator as the world becomes transformed into an Eden, to replace the one that was lost 6,000 years earlier. Speaking of the new age, Yahweh Elohim spoke these words to Isaiah:

"And though the Lord gives you the bread of adversity and the water of affliction, yet your teachers will not be moved into a corner anymore, but your eyes shall see your teachers. Your ears shall hear a word behind you saying, 'This is the way, walk in it,' whenever you turn to the right hand or whenever you turn to the left" (Isaiah 30:20-21).

God's people, the resurrected saints, will truly be shepherds in the new age, teaching people in the various nations the truths of living successful, abundant lives based on the laws of the Eternal

The effect of encouragement towards others in the face of trials is amazing, for it grants hope to the weak and weary, and accomplishment and success to those who are struggling to just make it through the day.[31]

dwelling within them. In John 10:11 and 14, Jesus is quoted, "I am the good Shepherd, and I know My sheep, and am known by My own." What is said about God's people as being shepherds? Quite a lot! Take a look at Acts 20:28.

> "Therefore take heed to yourselves and to all the flock, among which the holy spirit has made you overseers, to shepherd the church of God which He purchased with His own blood."

overseer = episkopos, "an inspector, an overseer, a watcher, guardian."[30]

Note that there is no indication here of the overseer being a dominant overlord, but he is a helper, an uplifter, a servant of the brethren of which he is one. As Paul stated in II Corinthians 1:24, "Not that we have dominion over your faith, but are fellow workers for your joy; for by faith you stand."

dominion over = kurieuo, "to be lord over, mastery over."[31]

faith = pistis, "faith, belief, from persuasion."[32]

Paul was at Miletus, having sent for the elders [older members] of the ecclesia at Ephesus, and when they had assembled he made them aware of their need to be watchmen and guardians — shepherds — of the brethren in Ephesus (Acts 20:17), since there would be wolves that would come along after he left, teaching false doctrines and trying to lead

brethren after themselves (Acts 20:29-30). THESE ELDERS WERE MADE OVERSEERS BY GOD'S SPIRIT — IT SAYS NOTHING ABOUT HANDS HAVING BEEN LAID ON THEM — TO LOVINGLY WATCH OVER AND GUARD THE YOUNGER BRETHREN FROM FALSE DOCTRINES, SINCE THESE OLDER BRETHREN [ELDERS] WERE MORE EXPERIENCED IN LIFE AND ABLE TO ACT AS SHEPHERDS.

The point made here is quite obvious. Older members of the ecclesia, through the action of the spiritual gifts imparted to them, are qualified to be shepherds, and are declared so by Paul. They can faithfully shepherd the flock and help guide — not domineer — the younger, less experienced brethren through troublesome situations. It is God's way: all of his elect gain experience from age and circumstances in life they face, and serve as guides within the flock. We may indeed generalize here and claim that ALL ELDERS ARE SHEPHERDS IN GOD'S ECCLESIA, especially those who labor in word and doctrine. These older brethren who 'rule well" should be counted worthy of double honor (I Timothy 5:17).

Peter supports Paul's view of the older people of the congregations being shepherds, when he said,

> "The elders who are among you I exhort, I who am a fellow elder and a witness of the sufferings of Christ, and also a partaker of the glory that will be revealed: shepherd the

flock of God which is among you, serving as overseers, not by compulsion but willingly, not for dishonest gain but eagerly; not as being lords over those entrusted to you, but being examples to the flock" (I Peter 5:1-3).

Peter continues his discussion by showing that all of the brethren are to be subject to one another, and in particular the younger people are to submit to the older brethren. While all are brothers in Christ, there is the need of the younger saints to show respect to those who are older and wiser.

You Older Brethren, Be Shepherds!

Thus, we have shown through Scripture that the older people amongst the elect are to be shepherds of others, and in a real sense WE ARE ALL TO SHEPHERD ONE ANOTHER, FOR WE ARE ALL TO BE SUBJECT ONE TO ANOTHER (Ephesians 5:21; I Peter 5:5). This subjection extends to the younger as well as the older members, but the older brethren, because of their accumulated wisdom, knowledge, and understanding, have the added responsibility of helping guide the younger members of the elect through a tumultuous world. We are all to serve one another with the gifts of the spirit that God has given each of us (I Peter 4:10; Romans 12:4-8; I Corinthians 12).

Perhaps the biggest stumbling block to the correct understanding of this concept of being a shepherd is the idea that an elder is someone who has been granted an office in the ecclesia by the laying on of hands. Such an idea is patently false, for the word for elder as used in the New Testament, *presbyteros,* means an older person, and nothing more. Sometimes older brethren have hands laid on them to show recognition that they have a certain job to do for a certain period of time, but an elder is not an office holder. *Elder* is merely an age designation, and in Scripture is used for those both inside and outside of the ecclesia.

We desperately need to support one another within the ecclesia so we can endure to the end (Matthew 24:13). We all have a responsibility to build up one another, especially as we see the end of the age approaching quickly.

Living God's government means shepherding one another. It is a major focus of love for our Creator and for one another. Let us internalize that wonderful way of relating to our brethren and express the love that the Prince of Peace has shown towards us!

God's government involves shepharding those in need of understanding, especially younger people who are growing in the faith and crave to understand the words of life.[35]

Joseph was placed into a pit by his brothers, and then sold to traders who brought him to Egypt, where he became second in command only to Pharaoh. Though esteemed least by his brothers, yet in the end he became first in authority and power.[1]

THE SIXTH BRANCH

LOVE IS
THE LEAST BEING THE GREATEST,
& THE LAST FIRST

The sons of Jacob, except for Joseph, Jacob's favorite, guided their father's flock to Shechem where lush pastures would provide excellent grazing. Jacob was interested in their welfare, so sent Joseph to investigate. The sons then went on further to Dothan, where Joseph caught up with them … and not being a favorite of any of them (for he had told them of dreams he had experienced where they all bowed down to him), they schemed to kill their youngest brother.

"Come therefore, let us now kill him and cast him into some pit; and we shall say, 'Some wild beast has devoured him.' We shall see what will become of his dreams!" (Genesis 37:20).

Reuben, however, wanted to save him and have him cast into a pit, where he could return later, extract him, and return him to his father. So the brothers stripped Joseph of his colorful tunic and cast him into a nearby dry pit, and shortly thereafter noticed a passing caravan of Midianite traders, to whom they sold Joseph. Reuben had left his brothers for a time, and later returned after the sale of Joseph, only to find his younger brother gone. This deeply distressed him, but the evil deed had been done and there was nothing he could do. Then all of the brothers decided to kill a goat and dip Joseph's tunic in its blood. This they presented to their father Jacob, who was overcome with grief over the supposed death of his favorite son. He could not be consoled. Read the story in Genesis 37.

Meanwhile, Joseph was sold by the Midianite traders to Potiphar, an officer of Pharaoh in Egypt, and we know well the rest of the story. Joseph was blessed by God and gained great favor in the eyes of Potiphar, who set him as overseer of all that he had. Then Potiphar's wife tried to seduce him, but Joseph would have none of such evil — Jacob had taught him the commandments of God — and was falsely accused of trying to rape the woman. That landed Joseph in prison, where he remained for two years until he was able to interpret the Pharaoh's dream of seven years of plenty followed by seven years of famine. Joseph was made second in command throughout all of Egypt, and engineered the storing of grain and other foodstuffs during the plentiful years, to prepare for the coming seven-year drought.

Amidst the great dearth, Joseph's brothers were sent by their father to Egypt to purchase grain where they met Joseph — whom they did not recognize— who put them through various tests and eventually had them and his father Jacob and their entourage move to Goshen in the Delta of the Nile River. There they lived and prospered under the guiding hand of Almighty God. See Genesis 39 to 47 for the full story.

This story of Joseph's demise and his being raised to power and authority is about as riveting and exciting as one can get! The last shall be first. A young man about to be murdered by his jealous brothers is sold into slavery, then elevated to the pinnacle of power of a major world empire in just a few years. The entire scenario is a tribute to the benevolence and power of the great God who has performed that same miracle over and over again for each one of us. Paul articulated the situation so eloquently in I Corinthians 1:26-29.

"For you see your calling, brethren, that not many wise according to the flesh, not many mighty, not many noble, are called. But God has chosen the foolish things of the world to put to shame the wise, and God has chosen the weak things of the world to put to shame the things which are mighty; and the base things of the world and the things which are despised God has chosen, and the things which are not, to bring to nothing the things that are, that no flesh should glory in His presence."

Jesus Christ made it plain that those who have been rejected by this society — "everyone who has left houses or brothers or sisters or father or mother or wife or children or lands, for My name's sake" — will receive a hundredfold in return, and ultimately eternal life …. "But many who are first will be last, and the last first (Matthew 19:29-30)." Let us take a close look at how the Eternal views all of His creations, made in His image, so He is able to say that the first will be last and the last will be first … that the greatest will be least and the least will be greatest.

1. God is no respecter of persons, but judges perfect judgment. "Do not judge according to appearance, but judge with righteous judgment" (John 7:24).

2. He directly states that the first will be last, and the last will be first (Matthew 19:30; 20:16; Mark 9:35; 10:31; Luke 13:30). Note carefully the parable of the workers in the vineyard in Matthew 20:1-16:

"For the kingdom of heaven is like a landowner who went out early in the morning to hire laborers for his vineyard. Now when he had agreed with the laborers for a denarius a day, he sent them into his vineyard. And he went out about the third hour and saw others standing idle in the marketplace, and said to them, 'You also go into the vineyard, and whatever is right I will give you.' So they went. Again he went out about the sixth and the ninth hour, and did likewise. And about the eleventh hour he went out and found others standing idle, and said to them, 'Why have you been standing here idle all day?' They said to him, 'Because no one hired us.' He said to them, 'You also go into the vineyard, and whatever is right you will receive.' So when evening had come, the owner of the vineyard said to his steward, 'Call the laborers and give them their wages, beginning with the last to the first.' And when those came who were hired about the eleventh hour, they each received a denarius. But when the first came, they supposed that they would receive more; and they likewise received each a denarius. And when they had received it, they complained against the landowner, saying, 'These last men have worked only one hour, and you made them equal to us who have borne the burden and the heat of the day.' But he answered one of them and said, 'Friend, I am doing you no wrong. Did you not agree with me for a denarius? Take what is yours and go your way. I wish to give to this last

The workers hired last to work in the vineyard were paid the same amount for the day's work as those hired first. This may seem unjust from a human point of view, but in God's eyes this is entirely just, for whether we are called early or late in life, our reward is the same, and it is infinite.[2]

man the same as to you. Is it not lawful for me to do what I wish with my own things? Or is your eye evil because I am good?' So the last will be first, and the first last. For many are called but few are chosen."

Let us review the parable. The vineyard owner hired laborers for the vineyard to begin work about daybreak, some hired at 9:00 a.m., some at noon, and some at 3:00 p.m. Then he began looking for workers at 5:00 p.m., an hour before sunset, and when he found some standing idle, he asked them, "Why have you been standing here idle all day?" They replied, "Because no one has hired us." Then the owner told them, "You also go into the vineyard, and whatever is right you will receive." At evening the owner had the steward call all of the workers to assemble to receive their wages, and he gave them all the same wage, a denarius.

We might say that logic would require for those who had worked longer hours in the vineyard to receive more than those who had worked only an hour. The owner of the vineyard then stated something as profound as it is revolutionary: "Friend, I am doing you no wrong. Did you not agree with me for a denarius? Take what is yours and go your way. I wish to give to this last man the same as to you …. So the last will be first, and the first last. For many are called, but few chosen."

The denarius is given to each worker: eternal life. Whether called early in life or late in life, fifty years before death, or just an hour before death, the reward is the same. For that fact we ought to rejoice, for what is a lifetime or an hour when compared to eternity as a spirit? The mere fact of entering God's kingdom ought to be reward enough. The destitute, poor widow and the rich evangelist get an equal reward: eternal life!

3. One's reward as a spirit is exactly what God decides, and it is in line with what he has made of us. This is confirmed by several scriptures.

> "And behold, I come quickly, and My reward is with Me, to give every man according as his work shall be" (Revelation 22:12).

The statements, "… the dead were judged out of those things which were written in the books, according to their works" (Revelation 20:12, 13; Romans 2:6), ought to be rendered as written above, "according as his work [in God's kingdom] shall be, because no amount of works can grant eternal life. It is a gift given by the Creator (Romans 6:23; 2:17), and our own righteousness is like filthy rags (Isaiah 64:6). We cannot "work up" salvation, but it is by God's *grace* [*charis*, "graciousness or favor"; from *chairo*, "to be cheerful, i.e. calmly happy or well-off"][3] that we are saved (Ephesians 2:5, 8; II Timothy 2:9). This last scripture in II Timothy 2:9 makes plain that God …

"... has saved us and called us with a holy calling, not according to our works, but according to His own purpose and grace which was given to us in Christ Jesus before the world began."

Note also what I Corinthians 12:18 states: "God has set the members, each one of them, in the body just as He pleased." Thus, our spiritual gifts, given to us by His spirit at baptism and the laying on of hands, are uniquely patterned to each one of us in terms of what God desires us to be. I would liken these spiritual gifts to "spiritual DNA" complementary to our physical DNA, which work together to grant unto us the qualities of being the arms, legs, head, heart, ears, fingers, or other parts of the spiritual body which together make for a whole, vibrantly functioning and adept at carrying out the work of teaching, prophesying, healing, administrating, helping, speaking in tongues, interpreting tongues, and expressing these gifts as apostles, prophets, teachers, healers, miracle workers, and whatever other manifestation the spirit desires.

4. Our Father in heaven has promised to make us all kings and priests (Exodus 19:6; I Peter 2:9; Revelation 1:6; 20:6; 22:5; Revelation 5:10), on an equal par, for a righteous Father will not play favorites with any of us (Leviticus 15:15; II Chronicles 19:7; Acts 10:34; Romans 2:11; Colossians 3:25). We are all equally loved by Him (Romans 5:8; 8:39; Ephesians 2:4; 5:2; I Thessalonians 2:16; I John 3:1, 16; 4:9-12, 16), for He made us, and we are sons made in His image (I John 3:1; Genesis 1:26-27; John 1:12).

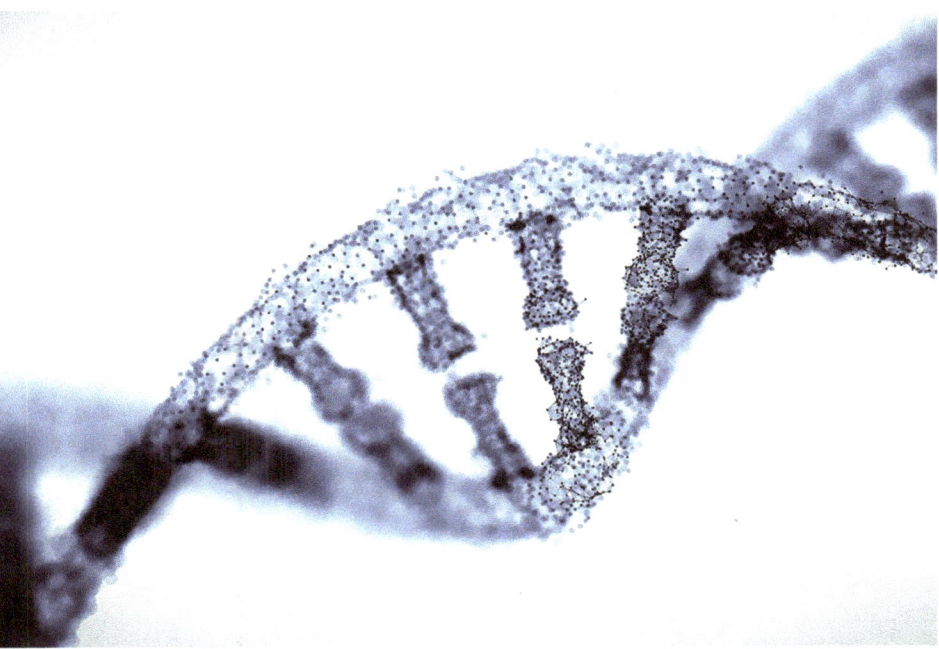

Like the DNA that defines our physical character that is present in each of the trillions of cells in our body, we might say that the spirit God places within us His "spiritual DNA" that defines what we are spiritually, especially in terms of the gifts that spirit brings with it.[4]

5. Our reward in the kingdom will be judged with perfect righteousness, based on our increase of the gifts and talents God has granted us. Notice this principle laid out neatly in Matthew 25:14-30 in the Parable of the Talents.

"For the kingdom of heaven is like a man traveling to a far country, who called his own servants and delivered his goods to them. And to one he gave five talents, to another two, and to another one, to each according to his own ability, and immediately he went on a journey. Then he who had received the five talents went and traded with them, and made another five talents. And likewise he who had received two gained two more also. But he who had received one went and dug in the ground, and hid his lord's money. After a long time the lord of those servants came and settled accounts with them. So he who had received five talents came and brought five other talents, saying, 'Lord, you delivered to me five talents; look, I have gained five more talents besides them.' His lord said to him, 'Well done, good and faithful servant; you were faithful over a few things, I will make you ruler over many things. Enter into the joy of your lord.' He also who had received two talents came and said, 'Lord, you delivered to me two talents; look, I have gained two more talents besides them.' His lord said to him, 'Well done, good and faithful servant; you have been faithful over a few things, I will make you ruler over many things. Enter into the joy of your lord.' Then he who had received the one talent came and said, 'Lord, I knew you to be a hard man, reaping where you have not sown, and gathering where you have not scattered seed. And I was afraid, and went and hid your talent in the ground. Look, there you have what is yours.' But his lord

Increasing our talents, like a trader reaping his profits through honest exchange, by using those talents to serve others is a most critical task that all of us must perform, whether it be teaching, prophesying, healing, or administrating.[5]

answered and said to him, 'You wicked and lazy servant, you knew that I reap where I have not sown, and gather where I have not scattered seed. So you ought to have deposited my money with the bankers, and at my coming I would have received back my own with interest. Therefore take the talent from him, and give it to him who has ten talents. For to everyone who has, more will be given, and he will have abundance; but from him who does not have, even what he has will be taken away. And cast the unprofitable servant into the outer darkness. There will be weeping and gnashing of teeth.'"

We are those servants who have been granted the talents — our gifts of the spirit — "… to each according to his own ability." Jesus, the man traveling to a far country, departed after the resurrection to the Father's right hand (Romans 8:34; Colossians 3:1; Hebrews 8:1). Once He left, the servant who had received five talents immediately went to work and, through trading, produced five more. Likewise, the servant that had been given two talents traded and gained two more, doubling his gifts as had the servant with five talents. The servant receiving one talent, though limited in gifts, hid his talent in the earth; he refused to use it and increase it. Fear held him in its grasp, and he squandered his potential and future reward.

Upon the return of the traveling owner (Christ), He complimented those who had received the five and two talents for doubling their master's gift. Interestingly, both servants were highly commended for being faithful in a few things, and were promised to be made *ruler* [*kathistemi*, "to appoint a person to a position of responsibility"][6] over many things. They were promised the same reward in spite of being given different inherent gifts.

The servant who received only a single talent but failed to increase it, and hid it in the ground out of fear, was severely chastised. He was cast into the lake of fire and destroyed for not having grown with his talents and abilities … showing the imperative need for all of us to move forward in life and grow … grow in knowledge, wisdom, understanding, truth, faith, and all of the spiritual fruits (Galatians 5:22-23). We all must use our fruits and gifts granted through God's spirit at baptism and the laying on of hand, using them in service to our brethren: "But the manifestation of the spirit is given to each one for the profit of all" (I Corinthians 12:7). All of the creation cries out to reproduce, to increase! That applies to our gifts and fruits as well.

The Parable of the Minas in Luke 19:12-27 tells a parallel story to that of the talents. The meaning is very much the same. Let us not forget the fact that our heavenly Father has prepared a great *house* [*oikia*, "a house or abode"][7] for us, the heavenly Zion, the New Jerusalem, and within that heavenly Zion are many *mansions* [*mone*, "residences or places to stay"][8] (John 14:2-3). These mansions, besides meaning simply residences, can be extended to include responsibilities within those residences … our spiritual gifts given now, expanded in the spirit realm to super-being capability!

6. Our Creator requires us to be humble like He is humble. Love being "the least is the greatest" points directly to humility … that other difficult-to-understand concept. It is absolutely certain that you cannot be close to your heavenly Father unless you are humble. What does humble mean?

> "Thus says the Lord: 'Heaven is My throne, and earth is My footstool. Where is the house that you will build Me? And where is the place of My rest? For all those things My hand has made, and all those things exist,' says the Lord. 'But to this one will I look: on him who is poor and of a contrite spirit, and who trembles at My word'" (Isaiah 66:1-2; also quoted in Act 7:49).

> "The Lord is near to those who have a broken heart, and saves such as have a contrite spirit" (Psalm 34:18).

> "The sacrifices of God are a broken spirit, a broken and a contrite heart — These, O God, You will not despise" (Psalm 51:17).

Our heavenly Father is the Great One who, along with others in the family of Elohim, created the heavens, the earth, and the seas (Genesis 1; I Corinthians 8:6). In fact, Jesus Christ created all things, along with the Father, both visible and invisible (Colossians 1:17). Yet, CHRIST IS THE EPITOME OF HUMILITY, WHO TOOK THE POSITION OF A SERVANT AND GOT DOWN ON THE FLOOR AND WASHED THE DISCIPLES' FEET!

We can definitely say that the love of our heavenly Father cannot be expressed to any of us unless we approach Him with an attitude of *humility* [*tapeinoo*, "to make low, bring low"].[10] It is this humility that the gentile peoples so often excelled in more than did the Israelites, whom Paul indicated are grafted in to the tame olive tree … so often in place of the natural Israelite branches that were broken off due to their unbelief and stubbornness (Romans 11:17-24). What matters in regard to whom our great God extends His love is not genetics; it is faith in Jesus Christ.

> "For you are all sons of God though faith in Christ Jesus. For as many of you as were baptized into Christ have put on Christ. There is neither Jew nor Greek, there is neither slave nor free, there is neither male nor female; for you are all one in Christ Jesus. And if you are Christ's then you are Abraham's seed, and heirs according to the promise" (Galatians 3:26-29).

To become great we must become humble and "least," like little children, as three of the Gospels spell out so succinctly:

"Let the little children come to Me, and do not forbid them, for of such is the Kingdom of God. Assuredly I say to you, whoever does not receive the kingdom of God as a child will by no means enter it" (Luke 18:16-17; see also Matthew 19:14 and Mark 10:14-15).

We are those "little children," and young children are humble and innocent, not striving to vaunt themselves above others … oh, with a selfish nature for sure, but not prone to ruling over others. We are those servants of the Eternal Living God who, in order to be

Imagine the Creator of the earth and all things in it washing your feet! You, as Peter, may protest vehemently such actions, understanding how sinful and unworthy you are of such treatment. Yet, that is exactly how He treats us — in total, unfeigned love — despite our unworthiness.[9]

great, must be as the younger, "… and he who governs as he who serves. For who is greater, he who sits at the table or he who serves? Is it not he who sits at the table? Yet I am among you as the one who serves" (Luke 22:26-27).

A just, loving God calls whom He will (John 6:44), and if He has predestined someone from the foundation of the world to be a son (Ephesians 1:3-6), then that person will be placed within the realm of Elohim — comprising the New Jerusalem (Revelation 21:9-10) — as a brother of Jesus Christ (Romans 8:29), alongside Him at the Father's right hand at His throne (Revelation 3:21). God is no respecter of persons, and judges righteous judgment (John 7:24; II Timothy 4:8). He has placed within each of us the gifts He has desired through His spirit, the perfect complement to our own physical DNA, as it were. Our judgment as to worthiness for eternal life is already determined as a gift, not something any of us can work up within ourselves, to somehow gain a better position, when the "last will be first and the first will be last."

Our Creator turns this present world upside down! The works of hierarchies in this world are not even counted amongst those within the ecclesia. We will all be brothers and sisters in the spirit realm, just as they are now within the body of Christ, on an equal par with one another to shine equally in full spiritual light!

Our Father and Jesus Christ turn the government and ways of this world upside down, bringing the humblest of us, those having no notoriety, into the highest of positions within His realm. It is like turning the pyramid of power in this world on its head![11]

What, then, is the incentive to produce good works if we are not given some sort of "extra reward or position" that elevates us above other? That question misses the entire point. What is greatness anyway? Is it not to wash the feet of your brother? Is it not to kneel on the floor, remove the dirty sandals of your brother, dip his feet in clean water, and wash them? Indeed! The least will be the greatest, and that is how our Father and Jesus Christ relate to us. That is how love is. Note the argument the apostles had on the night before Jesus' crucifixion, just after He had washed their feet, wondering who would be the greatest in the kingdom.

"And He said to them, 'The kings of the Gentiles exercise lordship over them, and those who exercise authority over them are called benefactors. But not so among you; on the contrary, he who is greatest among you, let him be as the younger, and he who governs as he who serves. For who is greater, he who sits at the table, or he who serves? Is it not he who sits at the table? Yet I am among you as the One who serves'" (Luke 22:25-27).

Are Positions Already Filled … Leaving No Place for You?

Some may wonder if there will be "important" positions for them in the new government of God on earth. We have already seen that "importance" is a term having no relevance amongst the saints in the new age. Everyone will have equal and incredible value as kings and priests, brothers of Jesus Christ, our Elder Brother both literally and figuratively washing the feet of each one of us! Whatever "positions" of responsibility we will be given will have no label of being "better" or "worse" than any other position, and very likely all will be in a place of similar responsibility since we will all

be kings and priests. Moreover, as sinless sons of God (I John 3:9), expressing flawlessly the fruits of the spirit, jealousy and competition over responsibilities will not exist, nor be possible. No one will be capable of lifting up his self-worth above someone else, for everyone will serve others in a foot washing attitude, looking upon others as better than themselves (Philippians 2:3).

What, then, of the promise the Savior gave to the twelve disciples who followed Him? After Peter asked Him what reward they would have by following Him, Jesus replied,

"Assuredly I say to you, that in the regeneration, when the Son of Man sits on the throne of His glory, you who have followed Me will also sit on twelve thrones, judging the twelve tribes of Israel" (John 14:2; see also Luke 22:30).

Just as Jesus spoke regarding the church of Laodicea, saying, "To him who overcomes I will grant to sit with Me on My throne, as I also overcame and sat down with My Father on His throne" (Revelation 3:21), so will the twelve apostles sit on His throne, as will all of the saints. Thus, in John 14:28 the phrase "… you who have followed Me will sit on twelve thrones …" is referring to not just the twelve but to all of us! There is no respect of persons with the Father in heaven and with our Elder Brother Jesus Christ.

This truth is in stark contrast to the

understanding of government by Herbert W. Armstrong who, in his book *Tomorrow … What It Will Be Like* (Everest House Publishers, New York, 1979, page 54), wrote the following about his vision of a coming hierarchy:

> "King David, resurrected, immortal, in power and glory, will be king, under Moses, over all twelve nations of Israel (Jeremiah 30:9; Ezekiel 34:23-24; 37:24-25). Each of the original twelve apostles will be king, under David, over one of these then super prosperous [Israelite] nations (Matthew 19:28)."

Herbert Armstrong then went on to claim that, under the apostles, "… each new king over a great nation, will be the rulers over districts, states, shires, counties or provinces, and over cities." He did not understand the loving government of the Almighty as revealed in God's word, but went so far as to claim that he had restored proper government within the church. Sadly, he did not see that his ideas merely copied the world's system patterned after Satan the Devil's hierarchies, and in particular the theology of the Roman Catholic Church which he claimed to reject in so many ways.

Indeed, Jeremiah 30:9, Ezekiel 34:23-24, and Ezekiel 37:24-25 speak of King David being "… their prince forever," and "… king over them [Israel]." Do these references to King David really mean that David will be the prince of Israel, or do they mean something else? According to A.R. Fausset in *A Commentary On the Old and New Testaments*,[13] Ezekiel 24:23 is speaking of the "… one Shephard set over them, and He shall feed them, even My servant David." The reference is to Jesus Christ, the Son of David, even as stated so in John 10:14; "I am the good Shepherd." David means "beloved," and the Messiah was truly God's beloved Son (Isaiah 13:21; Matthew 3:17). Messiah is called David in Isaiah 4:3-4, Jeremiah 30:9, and Hosea 3:5, and he certainly was a type of the Messiah. *The Abingdon Bible Commentary*[14] affirms A. R. Fausset's view, that the northern (Israel) and southern (Judah) kingdoms will be joined together, and "They shall be one kingdom with one king, a new David." Likewise, F. C. Cook states in regard to Ezekiel 37:22-25, "The restoration of Israel to their native soil will lead the way to the coming of the promised King, the Son of David …."[15]

What of the 144,000 in Revelation 7:4-8 who were sealed on their foreheads, 12,000 out of each of the twelve tribes … except Dan? Do they have the "inside track" and preclude any outside this elite group of saints from positions in the government of God? While these saints are indeed special in some way, note that in Revelation 7:9-17 another huge group of saints is mentioned,

> "… a great multitude that no one could number out of all nations, tribes, peoples,

and tongues, standing before the throne and before the Lamb, clothed with white robes, with palm branches in their hands...."

Verse 14 states that this huge multitude of saints came out of the Great Tribulation and was made white in Christ's blood, and serve

At the marriage supper of the Lamb in heaven, the resurrected saints will be given white robes, typifying righteousness ... unable to sin any more. They will all be equal in the eyes of the Father, and all equally brothers of Jesus Christ. As contrasted to this world, the last will be first, and the first last.[12]

God day and night in His temple (verse 15). So, we have a huge group of individuals who have been raised to eternal life and have been granted responsibilities in the City of God, at the Father's throne, like the rest of the saints who are raised at Christ's coming (I Corinthians 15:50-52; I Thessalonians 4:16-17). The significance of this 144,000 is not made clear, but they are in the eyes of God not more important than the great multitude mentioned in verse 9 ... nor are they any more important or occupy positions of greater responsibility than any of us will. God is no respecter of persons, and the concept of being "greater than" or "lesser than" another son is absent to a Father whose love for each of His children transcends our understanding.

The least will be the greatest and the greatest the least. The last will be first and the first will be last. These concepts are inherent within the mind of God and His plan for all of His people, and He will carry out this reality to the full ... because He loves us.

Oneness in marriage is a profoundly beautiful thing, exemplifying the very fabric of design for families as the Creator intended. When conflicts arise they must be dealt with according to His designs.[2]

THE SEVENTH BRANCH

LOVE IS THE FOUNDATION OF MARRIAGE

So many marriages break up after months or years of husband and wife living together. More and more people forego marriage altogether, not understanding the requirement for it within God's moral code, to bring up children in a stable and loving environment … and reap the unpleasant rewards of breaking the precepts upon which mankind is designed to thrive. Yet, a correct understanding of love can bring a husband and wife together even when challenged to the limit by the sins of the world. Here is one example.[1]

Watching his back disappear through our bedroom door, I wondered if he meant it this time. We'd often been challenged by conflicting schedules and discipline differences concerning our two pre-teen sons. Although our marriage had weathered many storms, lately I'd begun to feel as if our boat was sinking.

I sat on our bed and stared out the window. The sturdy cherry trees and tall pines reminded me of God's protection. If he could care for those landmarks, surely he'd protect our family. But I recalled how a violent summer storm had cost us three trees — a reminder that sometimes the worst of nature gets the best of us.

"We're incompatible. We should never have gotten married." Shocked, I returned to the house. I could only pray, "God, we need your help."

Finally, I walked downstairs and found Ted hunched over his computer — one of my regular complaints about him. The kids were playing next door, so we could talk openly. Placing an arm around his shoulders, I whispered, "I'm sorry."

Only recently had I begun to realize how my cutting words about his "inadequacies" as a husband and father had deeply wounded him. Barely glancing up, he replied, "That's not enough anymore. Nothing ever changes."

Feeling foolish, I withdrew my arm. "That's not true," I snapped. "I've changed over the past 10 years. You even said so."

Catching myself in defensive mode, I stopped mid-sentence and paused. "What would you like me to do?"

He sighed. "We've been through this before. If you don't know, I'm not telling you."

Thinking back over our married life, I recalled Ted's irritation on several occasions when he came home to a dark kitchen and no dinner as I spent hours on the phone cold-calling potential clients to jump-start a home business. Ted worked hard all day and wanted hot meals when he arrived home. He also wanted me to handle the kids' discipline immediately instead of waiting for him to get home, but I felt they needed his manly leadership. Slowly I was learning to let go of my way and trust God with his, but often I fell short, complaining because I had to lead family devotions when Ted was busy. Competing interests had drawn us away from each other. I realized guiltily that even the kids were uncomfortably aware of escalating tensions between us.

Interrupting my thoughts, he added, "I haven't loved you for a long time, and I'm not going to live like this for the next 50 years."

His words felt as if he'd punched me in the stomach. Shocked, I left his office in tears. It was one thing to be reminded of neglected duties; it was another to be told your spouse doesn't love you.

Hope withered with the late summer foliage. In a desperate attempt to salvage our marriage, I saw a Christian marriage counselor. Youthfully zealous, she incited me to action.

"Perhaps a divorce is best."

I couldn't believe what I was hearing. A Christian counselor was advising me to get divorced.

"I can't divorce Ted," I said. "That would hurt our kids. Besides, he'll start another life if I let him go now."

"Why not separate for a few months to clear the air?"

Though I wanted to dismiss the idea, I agreed to consider it.

Meanwhile, I was invited to teach at a conference in England later that fall. How ironic, I thought, that I, a communication expert and Christian, am contemplating marital separation. Perhaps God had engineered the conference to provide a short-term separation of his devising rather than a longer, man-made one. I'd be gone a week.

The day I received the invitation, I found Ted in the garage, hunting for a screwdriver. He barely looked up as I asked coyly, "Will you miss me when I leave?"

He replied far too calmly, "You better get an attorney. Mine is starting divorce proceedings."

"But we have to separate first!" I exclaimed.

"Whatever," he said shortly. "The attorneys can handle it."

"Is this about my criticizing your lack of family leadership?"

"We're incompatible. We should never have gotten married."

Shocked, I returned to the house. I could only pray, "God, we need your help."

Calming myself, the next day I called an attorney who agreed to represent me. I e-mailed Ted the attorney's contact information, too hurt to discuss it in person. A few days later I received a letter with the hearing date. The words stared at me from the page in an accusatory manner.

Was this my fault? I wondered. What would happen to our family?

My presentation on gender communication on England went well; too bad it wasn't helping at home. If only Ted and I could try again. If only … the two loneliest words in the universe.

The sorrow of death and the joy of living urged me to fight for my marriage. On the return flight I prayed earnestly, "God, thank you for showing me beauty and loss, joy and pain. Help me respond to Ted as I should. Life is short, and love is precious; help me savor both."

Arriving home at midnight, I peeked in on the sleeping boys. As I crept into bed beside my husband, he briefly stirred to mumble sleepily, "Glad you made it home okay."

My heart raced to think that his heart might be softening!

The next day after Ted came home from work, I found him in our bedroom changing clothes. "Can I talk to you a minute?"

"Go ahead," he said indifferently.

"I had time to think about us when I was in England. God helped me realize how much you and the boys really mean to me. I don't want anything to tear us apart."

"I don't know …" Ted began.

"Look," I interjected, "Philippians 4:13 says we can do all things with God who gives us strength. I'm committed to a fresh start in honoring our marriage and you. I'll do whatever it takes. But you have to work with me."

Taking a step toward him, I said, "We loved each other once. I apologize for my mistakes. I haven't respected your needs, and I've complained too often. I want to be a good wife."

After a moment, Ted said, "I'm sorry too. I've done and said things to you that I'm not proud of. I've made a lot of mistakes too. But what makes this time different? We'll just do the same things over again."

"Only God can make it different," I said. "I know I need to focus on strengthening my faith first. I plan to read my Bible every day, and I'm going to join a women's Bible study."

He started to move, and just when I thought he'd leave the room, he drew me into his arms. We cried as we clung to each other several minutes.

"I'll find a men's study," he whispered. "Maybe if I grow in my faith too."

We canceled that divorce hearing seven years ago, and all of us have become more grounded in the Bible and bonded to other believers. We even host a home Bible study. And yes … we're in love again. We learned that Philippians 4:13 holds truth: we can do all things through Christ who gives us strength.

This true story of a husband and wife at odds with each other shows that even seemingly hopeless conflicts can be turned around to yield loving and intensely fulfilling marriages. Marriage is the foundational institution upon which civilization is built. Marriage epitomizes the lifelong commitment that a man and a woman make to each other, to become a single functioning unit with the husband being the head and the wife the helpmate. It is a profound relationship designed and built around the very essence of love in all of its names: agape, philia, and eros combined to produce a unique oneness that is shared by no other two human beings on earth.

Marriage also is the oneness that epitomizes the union of Jesus Christ and the ecclesia, the marriage of Him with the saints at the resurrection:

"But I want you to know that the head of every man is Christ, the head of the woman is man, and the head of Christ is God [the Father]" (I Corinthians 11:3).

A properly tended husband-wife team is the very image of the heavenly, and the foundation of harmonious joy and accomplishment as the Creator intended.[3]

We will get into "headship" in a moment, but first let us examine the Biblical meanings of marriage.

Old Testament. There are relatively few citations concerning marriage, a few of which are mentioned here.[4] *laqach* = "to take, receive, take away, grasp, take hold of, take to oneself" (Genesis 19:14). This is the first occurrence of the word marriage in Scripture. *ownah* = "to dwell together, sexual cohabitation" (Exodus 21:10). *chathan* = "to give [a daughter] away in marriage; hence, to contract affinity by marriage" (Genesis 34:9; Deuteronomy 7:3).

baal = "to be master; hence, to marry"
(Proverbs 30:23;
Isaiah 54:1; 62:5; Jeremiah 3:14).

New Testament.[5]
gameo = "to wed" (Matthew 22:25;
Mark 10:12; I Corinthians 7:9).
ginomai = "to become, to come into existence"
(Romans 7:3).
ekgamizo = "to marry off a daughter"
(Matthew 22:30; 24:38; 25:10).

As we read in the chapter on Jesus Christ's revelation of love, there are other words that are translated as "love" in both testaments, such as *ohab* and *ahabah* (Hebrew),[6] and *storge*, *philautos*, and *xenia* (Greek).[7] The meanings of these words are very close to *ahab*, *agape*, and *phileo* in their contexts. Marriage implies a cleaving or grasping unto something, like marrying two different metals to make a strong alloy. Marriage is the binding of a male and female to become a strong, indissoluble unit that cannot be moved, even as the marriage of Jesus Christ and the elect is a perfect, whole, immovable unit. So is the union of the Father and the Son as indicated in I Corinthians 11:3. It is the oneness imputed to our original parents Adam and Eve in the Garden of Eden, wherein a portion of the man was removed, out of which was fabricated the woman to be his counterpart.

Adam was created as flesh and blood without a female companion, but soon loneliness overtook him, so the Creator made him a helpmate. It is not good for man to be alone; the man and woman make a complete unit.[8]

"Therefore a man shall leave his father and his mother and be joined to his wife, and they shall become one flesh" (Genesis 2:24).

This marriage was designed to be forever, as reinforced by Jesus when He was asked by the Pharisees if it is lawful to divorce a wife for any reason. He exclaimed,

"Have you not read that He who made them at the beginning made them male and female, and said, 'For this reason a man shall leave his father and mother and be joined to his wife, and the two shall become one flesh.' So then, they are no longer two but one flesh. Therefore, what God has joined together let not man separate" (Matthew 19:4-6).

Jesus made clear that, though Moses permitted divorce because of the hard, unloving hearts of the Israelites, such divorce did not exist in the beginning. Only because of sexual immorality was divorce permitted, and if divorce occurred for any other reason, then the person who married the divorced woman became an adulterer (Matthew 19:8-9). Clearly, marriage is to be permanent, and between one man and one woman for life. If either the husband or wife leaves the union for some reason other than adultery, and they are of the elect, they are to remain married though living separately (I Corinthians 7:10-11). Also, if a mate dies when both are of the elect, the living mate is free to marry someone in the faith (I Corinthians 7:39), in order that there be unity and love within the spirit that binds them together.

We have seen that the husband is to be the *head* of the wife, as Christ is the head of the ecclesia and the Father the *head* of Christ. This headship is emphasized in Ephesians along with the instruction that the wife be submissive to the husband.

"Wives, submit to your own husbands, as to the Lord. For the husband is the head of the wife as also Christ is head of the church, and He is the Savior of the body. Therefore, just as the church is subject to Christ, so let the wives be to their own husbands in everything" (Ephesians 5:22-24; see also Colossians 3:18; Titus 2:5; I Peter 3:1).

The word *head* in Greek is *kephale*, which means the head as a body part, but metaphorically the word shows the relationship of the Father, Christ, and the man and woman to one another. This relationship is emphatically based upon *love* (*agape*) of the one for the other, as made plain in Ephesians 5:25-33, which I will quote in its entirety due to the incredible emphasis that love and service — even sacrificing one's life for one's spouse — have within the concept of headship.

"Husbands, love your wives, just as Christ also *loved* [*agape*] the church and gave Himself for her, that He might sanctify and cleanse her with the washing of water by the word, that He might present her to Himself a glorious church, not having spot or wrinkle or any such thing, but that she should be holy and without blemish. So husbands ought to *love* [*agape*] their own wives as their own bodies; he who *loves* [*agape*] his wife loves himself. For no one ever hated his own flesh, but nourishes and cherishes it, just as the Lord does the church. For we are members of His body, of His flesh and of His bones. 'For this reason a man shall leave his father and mother and be joined to his wife, and the two shall become one flesh.' This is a great mystery, but I speak concerning Christ and the church. Nevertheless let each one of you in particular so *love* [*agape*] his own wife as himself, and let her see that she *respects* [*phobeo*, "be in awe of, revere"][10] her husband."

Notice how *agape* is intertwined with the whole idea of headship, showing that to be the head is to be a loving, serving, protecting, and uplifting companion who is willing to literally sacrifice his life, as well as his time and energy, for the apple of his eye. What an incredibly beautiful and functional relationship marriage is designed to be!

This loving relationship between the husband and wife is applauded in Proverbs 5:18-19, not just with *agape* love but also with erotic love as designed within the marriage covenant.

"Let your fountain be blessed, and rejoice with the wife of your youth. As a loving deer and a graceful doe, let her breasts satisfy you at all times; and always be enraptured with her love."

This physical attraction and fulfillment within marriage is further glamorized in Song of Solomon, where the physical attributes of the Shulamite woman are lauded, such as her overall appearance, mouth, breasts, cheeks, neck, eyes, hair, lips, skin, legs, and fragrance … everything a husband can physically appreciate in his wife. The Beloved is likewise praised for his handsomeness, strength, and great desire for her. The word *Shulamite* comes from the Hebrew word *shalam*, meaning "perfection and completion of a condition or action,"[12] and within the Song of Solomon we see the wooing of the Beloved (Solomon) of a shepherdess, and the joys and heartaches of wedded love. Allegorically the book pictures Israel as God's betrothed bride (Hosea 2:19-20), and the ecclesia as the bride of Christ. While

Even in older age the husband-wife team expresses the epitome of love, of caring for one another especially in difficult times, lifting one another up just as the Eternal does for each of His elect in times of trouble to support the future bride of His firstborn Son.[11]

physical life finds its greatest fulfillment in the love of a man for a woman — and vise-versa — so spiritual life finds its highest fulfillment in the love of God for His people, and of Christ for the ecclesia.

This marriage of Christ and the elect is prophesied to occur just after the resurrection (I Corinthians 15:51-52; I Thessalonians 4:15-17; Matthew 24:30-31), when the saints rise to meet Jesus in the air, are transported to the heavenly city, and meet the Father of the Bride at the marriage supper (Revelation 19:6-9). So, we see a close parallel between marriage within both the physical and spiritual planes. The oneness of the marriage partners in both cases is complete and forever. It is the "great mystery," I believe, that Paul talked about in Ephesians 5:32, which answers to John 17:21: "… that they all may be one, as You, Father, are in Me, and I in You; that they also may be one in Us …." What an incredible truth that is, a truth that describes the love the Creator has for His Son Jesus and for each of us! It is also the solution to the mystery that has been hidden from ages and generations, but now is made plain to us: "… Christ in you, the hope of glory" (Colossians 1:26-27).

A Closer Look at Marriage

Let us examine marriage in the physical realm and its integration of the agape, philia, and eros meanings of love.

What are the purposes of marriage?

1. Reproduce. Without producing children the species would cease to exist, and the command to be fruitful and multiply could not be fulfilled (Genesis 1:28; 9:1).

2. Express love between husband and wife. There is a vacant spot in the hearts of both a man and a woman that was designed to be filled only by one's true love … though God can fill that as well; note I Corinthians 7:25-35, and Christ's interesting statement in Matthew 19:10-12.

a. Notice in Genesis 2:19-23 that the woman was taken from the man, and the man naturally wants to have that female essence back with him.

b. Jacob was highly impressed with the lovely Rachel (Genesis 29:9-11, 16-20). Rachel was *beautiful* [*yapheh*, "bright"][13] in her figure or outline, and *well favored* [*mareh*][14] in her appearance, shape, comeliness, or view. Leah was *weak* [*rak*][15] in her appearance.

c. Elkanah loved Hannah, but also had a second wife named Peninnah (I Samuel 1:2-5). Interestingly, God blessed the unloved wives with more children than he did the loved wives.

3. Creation of a family environment in which to raise children of the next generation in the ways of Almighty God. This cornerstone of a loving, Godly family is designed to be the foundational building block of every civilization of man (Deuteronomy 6:6-9; Ephesians 6:1-4).

What are the rules protecting marriage?
Because of the incredible and central importance of marriage in the fulfillment of God's plan, it stands to reason that our Creator would have prepared safeguards to protect it. Indeed He has, and here are some of them.

1. **"You shall not commit adultery"** (Exodus 20:14). *Adultery* [*naaph*, "to commit adultery"][17] is the single most destructive act within marriage, which is akin to idolatry and shows one's intent to disregard the promises made at the marriage ceremony. It is the one allowance for divorce (Matthew 5:32). Actually, the word for *fornication* in

Along with marriage come children, the increase of the family, sons and daughters destined to expand the family of God of which increase there will be no end. Without this increase the human species would cease to exist.[16]

> W*ithout producing children the species would cease to exist, and the command to be fruitful and multiply could not be fulfilled. (Genesis 1:28; 9:1)*

Greek, as used in this verse, is *porneia*, and can mean any form of sexual looseness, harlotry, incest, bestiality, and so forth.[18]

2. **"You have heard that it was said by them of old time, you shall not commit adultery; but I say unto you that whosoever looks on a woman to lust after her has committed adultery with her already in his heart"** (Matthew 5:27-28). Jesus showed that even to *lust* [*epithumia*, "to set the heart upon, i.e. long for"][19] is

committing adultery. The attitude of purity of heart towards one's mate — the one and only — is critically important.

3. Marriage is so important to our Father that He set in place a whole set of laws to protect the marriage bond and discourage sexual impurity. See Deuteronomy 22:13-30, Leviticus 18; 20:10-22, and I Corinthians 5:1-13 for a start.

4. We are to marry within our race, even our tribe, and when in the ecclesia only to those who are also called-out ones.

a. Abram married Sarai (Genesis 11:29).
b. Isaac married Rebekah from the same home area (Genesis 24:3-4, 67).
c. Jacob married wives from the home area in Ur (Genesis 29:15-30).
d. Israelites were to marry within their own tribes, or at the very least marry other Israelites (Exodus 34:16; Leviticus 21:14; Deuteronomy 7:3-4; I Chronicles 23:22; Ezra 9:1-12; Nehemiah 10:30; 13:26-27; Malachi 2:11; I Corinthians 7:39; II Corinthians 6:14).

5. Sometimes parents selected mates for their children to insure good matches that immature young adults might not appreciate.

a. Hagar selected a wife for Ishmael (Genesis 21:21).
b. Abraham procured Isaac's wife (Genesis 24).
c. Laban arranged for his daughters' marriage (Genesis 29).
d. Samson asked that his parents get him a wife (Judges 14:2).
e. Parents' consent in some circumstances is required by the law (Exodus 22:17).

6. Celibacy as a doctrine is deplored (Judges 11:38; Isaiah 4:1; Jeremiah 16:9).

Men are attracted to women they consider beautiful, and such is the course of life which the Creator has set in force to assure that marriage and procreation would occur. How God brings about this attraction is a mystery, and can lead to fascinating consequences, such as with Jacob and Laban's daughters.[20]

How is marriage to be lived?

1. It is a joyous, loving union (Ecclesiastes 4:9-12). "Let your fountain be blessed: and rejoice with the wife of your youth. Let her be as the loving hind and pleasant roe; let her breasts satisfy you at all times, and be ravished always with her love" (Proverbs 5:18-19; see also Colossians 3:19).

2. The husband is to head the wife, and the wife is to submit, but each is to submit to the other. We have already seen Ephesians 5:22-23, but note verse 21. "Submitting yourselves one to another in the fear of God." See also Colossians 3:18-19.

3. Modesty, humility, and service to one another must be the rule in daily living. Notice the comments by Peter in I Peter 3:1-7.

"Likewise, you wives, be in subjection to your own husbands; that, if any obey not the word, they also may without the word be won by the conduct of the wives, while they behold your chaste conduct coupled with fear. Whose adorning let it not be that outward adorning of plaiting the hair, and wearing of gold, or putting on of apparel; but let it be the hidden man of the heart, in that which is not corruptible, even the ornament of a meek and quiet spirit, which is in the sight of God of great price. For after this manner in the old time the holy women also, who trusted in God, adorned themselves, being in subjection unto their own husbands; even as Sarah obeyed Abraham, calling him Lord, whose daughters you are as long as you do well, and are not afraid with any amazement. Likewise, you husbands, dwell with them according to knowledge, giving honor unto the wife as unto the weaker vessel, and as being heirs together

Now Laban had two daughters; the name of the older was Leah, and the name of the younger was Rachel. Leah had weak eyes, but Rachel had a lovely figure and was beautiful. Jacob was in love with Rachel, and said, "I'll work for you seven years in return for your younger daughter Rachel" (Genesis 29:16-18).

of the grace of life, that your prayers be not hindered."

4. The wife is to be virtuous and honorable, as is the husband (Proverbs 31:10-31; Hebrews 13:4; Ephesians 5:28).
5. Treat your spouse as you wish to be treated yourself (Matthew 7:12; Leviticus 19:18; Matthew 22:40; Romans 13:8-10; Galatians 5:14; I Timothy 1:5).

How is marriage not to be lived?
1. Contentions are to be avoided (Proverbs 21:9; 21:19).
2. Have only one wife or one husband.
   a. The kings were cautioned not to have many wives (Deuteronomy 17:17).
   b. Solomon was led astray by many wives (I Kings 11:3-4).
   c. A man of God must have one wife (I Timothy 3:2, 12; Titus 1:6; Genesis 2:22).

Marriage is under attack from many angles in today's world. It always has been, but now more than ever. With electronic media making pornography easily accessible, the sanctity of marriage is being besmirched. According to one source,

"Pornography is a social and physical toxin that destroys relationships, steals innocence, erodes compassion, breeds violence, and kills

A major consequence of a loving marriage is to raise children, thus multiplying those made in the express image of the Creator and fulfilling the command to "Be fruitful, multiply, and replenish the earth." [23]

love. The issue of pornography is ground zero for all those concerned for the sexual health and well-being of our loved ones, communities, and society as a whole."[21]

This resource site lists a multitude of problems throughout society caused by viewing pornography, and Jesus Christ directly warned us about looking lustfully at a woman; the same can be applied to women. The author gives sound advice, since viewing pornography leads to less satisfaction in sexual activity, begets loneliness, and greatly increases the chances for divorce. Revenues for pornography worldwide are well over $20 billion.[22]

The reasons for such attacks on marriage,

> "Marriage is designed to be the perfect combination of agape, philia, and eros aspects of love."

and love in general, should not be any surprise. Satan the devil is terribly angry and jealous with humanity and its ability to reproduce potential sons of Elohim. He cannot reproduce, and these sons of Elohim are destined to take over the realm he has so zealously controlled for 6,000 years … he being the god of this world (II Corinthians 4:4; Ephesians 2:2). He has done, and is doing, everything he can to besmirch the sanctity of marriage, destroy love within this most sacred union, and pervert the purity and blessings of sexual activity within marriage which produce more children. Satan himself is perverted, and he will do whatever it takes to spread around that perversion through education, radio and television, government, and the electronic media that he has subverted. He is the "prince of the power of the air" (Ephesians 2:2), and as such has done incredible damage to the purity of human minds relating to marriage and sexuality. Yet, his doom is coming, and he knows it. He will be destroyed in due course, but not without putting up a royal fight!

Our heavenly Father reveals what love is within marriage and the family. Marriage is designed to be the perfect combination of agape, philia, and eros aspects of love. This is a fact that even psychotherapists recognize, such as Viktor Frankl promotes with his logotherapy practice.[24] Let us carefully cultivate that wonderful relationship within our own homes, and thereby glorify the Creator God who made us in His image!

DO YOU KNOW WHAT I HAVE DONE TO YOU?

THE EIGHTH BRANCH

LOVE IS REVEALED IN THE CREATION

We tend to think of love in its various connotations only within the human realm, but if we stop there we are making a serious mistake. Love in its deepest sense is expressed throughout the created world, amongst people, animals, and even plants. After all, did not the Apostle Paul write in Romans 1:19-20,

> "… because what may be known of God is manifest to them, for God has shown it to them. For since the creation of the world His invisible attributes are clearly seen, being understood by the things that are made, even His eternal power and Godhead, so that they are without excuse."

"His invisible attributes …." This must surely include the attribute of love … the selfless care of one for another. Let us take a look at some vivid examples.

Dogs team up to save a drowning toddler[1]

They're tough breeds and they have the rough-and-tumble names to match. But free-spirited Aussie dogs Tank the Rottweiler-cross and Muck the Staffie-cross instinctively knew when a small child was in danger, and their protective natures averted a tragedy.

One December afternoon, Georgie Hillier thought her two-year-old son Max was playing in the back garden of their home in rural Queensland, Australia. But when she went to check, there was no sign of Max or their dog Tank. When she couldn't find them, she jumped in her car and started scouring the neighboring property. She was frightened her son could have fallen into one of the dams or reservoirs.

Then she found Tank with the neighbor's dog Muck. They were both running around the dams, barking furiously and covered in mud and slime. "I just panicked. I was running around, checking the sides of the dams," Georgie told Sara Hicks from radio station ABC Local. While she kept searching, a neighbor called the police. Eventually, a woman who had found Max heard Georgie's calls and brought the unharmed toddler out to her.

There was no one there to witness what exactly happened, but Michael Beattie from the Royal Society for the Prevention of Cruelty to Animals takes up the story. "When the police arrived on the scene, they saw quite distinct drag marks. It was apparent that young Max had actually been pulled out of the dam by one of the dogs — most likely Tank. Max was making moves to go back into the dam and Muck was virtually heading him off at the pass. It was the police's opinion that the only way that Max was rescued from drowning was by the two dogs."

A pod of dolphins protects a lifeguard and his family from sharks[2]

In late 2004, lifeguard Rob Howes and his family were out swimming at Ocean Beach, near Whangarei, New Zealand, when seven bottlenose dolphins approached and herded them together. "They were behaving really weird," Howes recalled, "turning tight circles on us, and slapping the water with their tails." He and his daughter's friend Helen had drifted about twenty meters away from his daughter and another friend before a dolphin swam straight at them and dived back down into the water before them.

"I turned in the water to see where it was

going to come up," Howes went on, "but instead I saw this great big grey fish (later revealed to be a great white shark) swim around me. It glided in an arc and headed for the other two girls. My heart went into my mouth because one of them was my daughter. The dolphins were going ballistic."

"The dolphins then herded the swimmers together and circled protectively around them for another forty minutes, fending off the shark." Dr. Rochelle Constantine from the Auckland University School of Biological Science said, "From my understanding of the behavior of these dolphins, they certainly were acting in a way which indicated the shark posed a threat to something. Dolphins are known for helping helpless things. It is an altruistic response, and bottlenose dolphins in particular are known for it."

A sea lion saves a young man who jumped off the Golden Gate Bridge[4]

California resident Kevin Hines knows that he is lucky to be alive after jumping off the Golden Gate Bridge in San Francisco, during a severe bout of mental illness. Here are the facts.

"On September 25, 2000, due to bipolar disorder and serious psychosis, I jumped off of the Golden Gate Bridge. I was nineteen years old, and after leaving the Bridge my first thought was that I had made a terrible mistake. Miraculously, I survived. Despite my severe injuries I was able to reach the surface of the water. Upon my resurfacing, I bobbed up and down in the frigid waters surrounding me. Then, something brushed by my legs. I feared it was a shark come to devour me whole. I tried to punch it thinking it might bite me. However, this marine animal just circled beneath me, bumping me up."

A passerby, who saw that the animal in question was a sea lion, quickly called for help. A rescue team was able to get to Kevin in time and pull him from the water, but it is doubtful that he would still be alive today had not the helpful sea lion kept his head above water.

Then there are cases that have been observed of one species of animal coming to the rescue of another species that is in dire danger.

Take the case of some humpback whales in Antarctica that teamed up to defend some seals that were close to being eaten for dinner by killer whales.

Humpback whales ward off killer whales from seals[5]

These are the words of marine ecologist Robert Pitman, who works for the National Oceanic and Atmospheric Administration in LaJolla, California.

"We were doing killer whale research in Antarctica and had the BBC on board filming *Frozen Planet*. We saw some killer whales interacting with some humpbacks and thought it could be an attack. We went over to have a

A humpback whale leaping from the water is a dramatic example of how the Creator has engineered life to not only enjoy itself in living, but also express the infinite talent of creation of life forms that shout forth His love to all who will see.[6]

look and the humpbacks were a little agitated, but it wasn't a full-on attack, and the killer whales ended up going away. We weren't quite sure what was going on, but when we looked at the BBC footage, we saw there was a Weddell seal between the two humpbacks. So we thought maybe the seal was trying to escape and found refuge.

"We followed the killer whales and soon they started attacking a crabeater seal on an ice floe, creating waves to try to wash it off. A few minutes later, the two humpbacks we had left behind came charging in and chased after the killer whales, slapping their flippers and making a nuisance of themselves. This was different because the humpbacks were on the offensive. But we figured it was just mobbing behavior, like when garden birds mob a predator to try to get rid of it.

"Well, a couple of days later we saw some killer whales attacking a Weddell seal on an ice floe and there were a couple of humpbacks in the vicinity. We could tell they were agitated because we could hear them bellowing — it's an impressive sound. The killer whales washed the seal off the ice and it started swimming into open water. Then, suddenly, one of the humpbacks comes to meet the seal and, just as it gets to the seal, rolls over on its back and the water washes the seal onto its chest. The whale lifts its chest up out of the water with the seal on it. We were amazed to see it. But we immediately thought maybe the whale didn't know the seal was there, maybe this was all just coincidence. Then we looked at the BBC footage, and we saw that at one point the seal had started to slip off the whale's chest. The humpback used a five-meter-long, one-tonne flipper to gently nudge the seal back up onto its chest. Once we saw that, we knew it was no accident and something was going on. It looked like altruism — as if the whales were acting out of concern for the smaller animal. But we are not talking about humans here, and when animals do something that appears to be altruism, I try to come up with rational explanations for it. But the reason wasn't obvious because, as best we know, animals always act in their own self-interest. This needs an explanation, I thought.

"It has taken a while to convince people. In the animal world, altruism is a thorny issue because it can be difficult to explain in terms of natural selection. While certain acts can look like they are driven by compassion, researchers are wary of attributing such feelings to animals. It's amazing how it raises hackles.

"So, are the whales being altruistic? If you define altruism as a behavior that increases the recipient's fitness at the cost of the performer's, then it's pretty clear that this is altruism. Humpbacks are coming in to drive off killer whales. That seems to be humpbacks acting against their own best interests."

Perhaps there is an underlying reason for humpback whales regularly fending off killer whales that relates to their survival, but no such reason was apparent in the ecologist's view. Are the humpback whales being truly altruistic ... or could we say selfless in helping their fellow friends, the seals, to survive against the attacks by vicious killer whales? This appears to be the case, and it has nothing to do with Darwinian evolutionary theory, but rather flies in the face of it.

We could further explore similar instances of one species protecting another in the animal kingdom, but let's shift to the plant kingdom for a bit. Is it possible that we can discover selfless love operating within the realm of our green-leafed friends of the grasslands and forests? Does the Apostle Paul's contention that the created world reveals God's nature, including the capacity to love selflessly, extend even to immobile plants?

Trees talk to each other

A German forester contends that trees — and by inference other plants — actually communicate with one another, an idea that is shaking up the scientific world. A writer discussing his finding in *Smithsonian Magazine*, Richard Grant, went so far as to say, "They're involved in tremendous struggles and death-defying dramas. To reach enormousness, they depend on a complicated web of relationships, alliances, and kinship networks. Wise old mother trees feed their saplings with liquid sugar and warn the neighbors when danger approaches. Reckless youngsters take foolhardy risks with leaf-shading, light-chasing, and excessive drinking, and usually pay with their lives. Crown princes wait for the old monarchs to fall so they can take their place in the full glory of sunlight. It's all happening in the ultra-slow motion that is tree time, so that what we see is a freeze-frame of the action."[7]

Peter Wohlleben is a German forester who for decades has managed a forest reserve, and has written a book *The Hidden Life of Trees: What They Feel, How They Communicate — Discoveries from a Secret World*.[8] In it he describes how trees are far more alert, social, sophisticated — and even intelligent — than we have thought. For instance, two old and majestic trees growing close to one another – "old friends" — carefully share the space above for their leaf canopies, and when one dies the other usually dies soon afterwards. The old Darwinian idea of "survival of the fittest" does not truly operate within the forest ecosystem, but rather trees are communal, and often form alliances with other species nearby. They share a collective intelligence like an insect colony, and are cooperative and interdependent.[9]

This interdependence is managed and expedited underground by a mycorrhizal fungi network, a vast array of fungal hyphae that form an intimate association with the roots, and using about 30% of the tree's photosynthetic energy grow out into the soil and extract essential nutrients like nitrogen, phosphorus, zinc, and copper, and channel them back to the tree roots for uptake. It is a dynamic mutualism, the fungi and the tree serving one another to the profit of each. Moreover, this hyphal network connects the tree roots underground so that smaller, shaded trees, lacking full sunlight to manufacture enough of their own food, are fed by the taller, stronger trees. As Wohlleben says, "The mother trees suckle their young."[10]

This tendency of a tree network to not abandon even its long-fallen "respected matriarchs" is evidenced by a broken stump, hundreds of years old, still having green chlorophyll in its remaining cambium. "Like elephants, they are reluctant to abandon their dead," says Wohlleben.[11]

Trees communicate through chemical, hormonal, and slow-pulsing electrical signals, the latter means similar to animal nervous systems, though without neurons. They also communicate through the air with pheromones and other odors. An acacia tree in the African Savannah, when grazed by a giraffe, will emit ethylene to warn nearby or downwind trees to produce tannins, which can sicken the animals. Trees can detect scents and in a sense taste substances through their leaves, sending signals to, for instance, attract caterpillar-consuming wasps once the caterpillar saliva is detected.

Other tree researchers concur with Peter Wohllenben, such as Suzanne Simard at the University of British Columbia in Vancouver. Her scientific approach to uncovering tree behavior departs from the dry prose of scientific writing, as she views the biggest and oldest trees of the forest as being nurturing, supportive, and

Perhaps no other soil organism expresses the love of God more than the mycorrhizae, which are fungi that extend from the roots into the soil around them and multiply the feeding volume of the roots, enabling them to search out nutrients and bring them to the roots for further growth. They are incredibly powerful servants of life.[12]

maternal. These matriarchs help their neighbors by sending them nutrients, and when these neighbors suffer distress the "mother tree" will increase the flow of nutrients.[13]

One of Dr. Simard's graduate students stated, "We don't know what they're saying with pheromones most of the time. We don't know how they communicate within their own bodies. They don't have nervous systems, but they can still feel what's going on, and experience something analogous to pain. When a tree is cut, it sends electrical signals like wounded human tissue." Peter Tompkins and Christopher Bird in *The Secret Life of Plants* pointed out that plants, like the purple passion plant, can respond to polygraph tests when threatened, and can pass these messages to surrounding plants as well, even when separated by distance and walls.[14]

So, can trees and plants show love to others? The evidence is that they can in selfless, altruistic ways. But let us not stop here, but move on to the unseen microbial world. Perhaps there are lessons to learn about love there as well.

Bacteria survive best among friends.

The "survival of the fittest" paradigm championed by Charles Darwin, and was a major part of his theory of evolution, has now been supplanted by new research that shows the "survival of the friendliest" is the reality in the bacterial world. Soren Sorensen and associates at the University of Copenhagen have studied how combinations of bacteria behave together when in a confined area. Thousands of different combinations have led them to conclude that bacteria cooperate to survive. As Sorensen states,

Bacteria and other organisms in soils, on skin surfaces, and elsewhere have been found to cooperate, showing that the "law of the jungle" is not what works best throughout the creation, but rather mutualism works best ... love towards one's neighbor.[21]

"In the classic Darwinian mindset, competition is the name of the game. The best suited survive and outcompete those less well-suited. However, when it comes to microorganisms, like bacteria, our findings reveal that the most cooperative ones survive."[15]

By forcing various bacterial species to grow together in a confined space, these microbiologists showed that instead of outcompeting one another while generating biofilms, bacteria allowed space for the weakest so they could grow better than they would have on their own. Furthermore, the different species split up laborious tasks by shutting down unnecessary mechanisms and sharing them with their neighbors.[17]

The cooperation of microorganisms and plant roots

The root zone (rhizosphere) of plants has

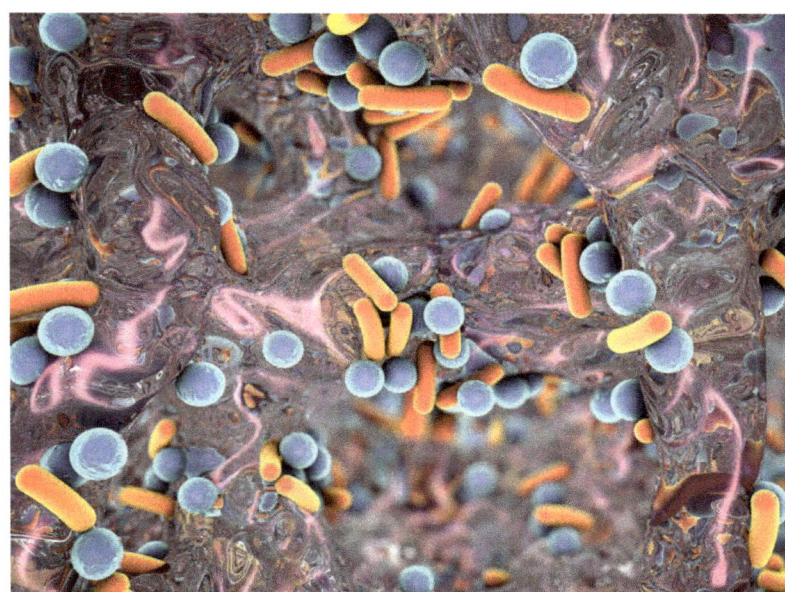

been a mystery during the history of mankind, until fairly recently when it was discovered that the surfaces of root hairs are populated by trillions of microorganisms. While thought to solely provide only anchorage and the uptake of nutrients and water — which of course they do — this new discovery made plain that plants do not feed these organisms for nothing. In fact, up to 50% of the plant's energy stores are moved from the leaves, down the phloem vessels, below the soil surface to grow roots, but moreover to excrete much of this carbohydrate energy into the soil itself outside the roots.[18]

There had to be some reason for this massive

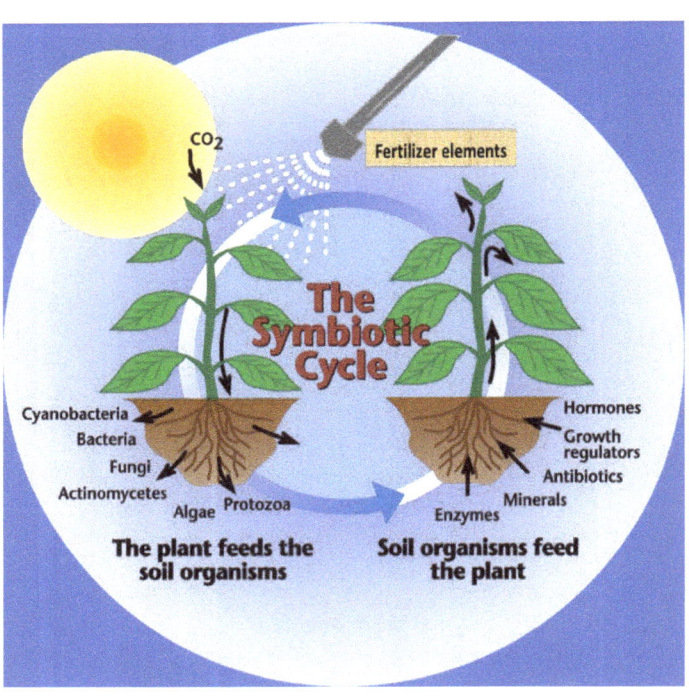

expense of energy donated to this exudation of energy … and indeed the reason was discovered. The sugars, proteins, and other compounds that are excreted from the root surfaces into the soil feed an incredible array of bacteria, fungi, algae, cyanobacteria, actinomycetes, and other organisms — both macro and micro — that in turn produce by-products very helpful to the plant.[19] These by-products include the following:

- Available nutrients for growth.
- Improved soil structure to ease the extension of roots, and enhance the movement of water and air to roots and the microbes themselves.
- Antibiotics for disease protection.
- Growth regulators and vitamins for growth stimulation
- Population of root surfaces with beneficial bacteria to fend off disease organisms.

In particular, the mycorrhizal fungi serve as a delivery system for nutrients to the roots, their filamentous hyphae setting up residence within root cells and proliferating out into the soil in a network that greatly expands the feeding volume of the root system. Most phosphorus the plant needs is extracted from the soil by these

Even plants and their functions express the love of the Creator. Root surfaces carry a huge population of bacteria, fungi, and other organisms that feed the plant through a mutualistic relationship which benefits both the microbes and the plant … which can be defined as love.[21]

filaments and delivered to the roots.[20] Besides, they take up water better than roots in drought and under salty soil conditions. They are marvels of the creation!

Thus, in every respect of the word the soil and microorganisms, in their mutualistic associations, show great love for one another, selflessly serving one another, each benefitting in dramatic ways. In fact, were it not for this association many plants would not survive, and the rest would do poorly. The "law of the jungle" does not dictate the health of plant ecosystems; it is the "law of cooperation and love" that makes our soils and plants prosper … and makes it possible for civilization to exist. The more we optimize this beautiful God-plane system, the better off all of us will be.

The human body … the epitome of love!

Of all the creations God has made, there is no other that compares with the human body. Made in the image of Elohim — God being love — therefore the human body pictures love in its fullness. How does it do that?

We learn directly from Hebrews that when God instructed Moses to build the Tabernacle in the Wilderness — the golden censor, golden pot, lampstand, table of showbread, veil, Ark of the Covenant, stone tables with the Ten Commandments, cherubim, and every other part of the tabernacle including the altar, fences, holy place, Holy of Holies, and even the priests and their garments and the sacrifices of blood offerings — all of these pictured the reality of unseen heavenly things.

"… for if He [Christ] were on earth, He would not be a priest, since there are priests who offer the gifts according to the law, who serve the copy and shadow of heavenly things …" (Hebrews 8:4-5).

"Therefore it was necessary that the copies of the things in the heavens should be purified with these, but the heavenly things themselves with better sacrifices than these. For Christ has not entered the holy places made with hands, which are copies of the true, but into heaven itself, now to appear in the presence of God for us …" (Hebrews 9:23-24).

The human body, being a picture of the very being of God, reveals to us His loving nature. Let us take a closer look at this most impressive human body and all that it is so we may perceive more intimately the love of our Creator. First, let us examine the cells which comprise the human body, of which there are around 10 trillion for the average person. Think of that: 10 trillion! These all began with a single cell, the ovum of the mother, which, when combined with the male sperm, began an astounding series of divisions that ended up producing the human body.

Even though there are several hundred cell types in the body, all of them can be grouped into just four main categories.[23]

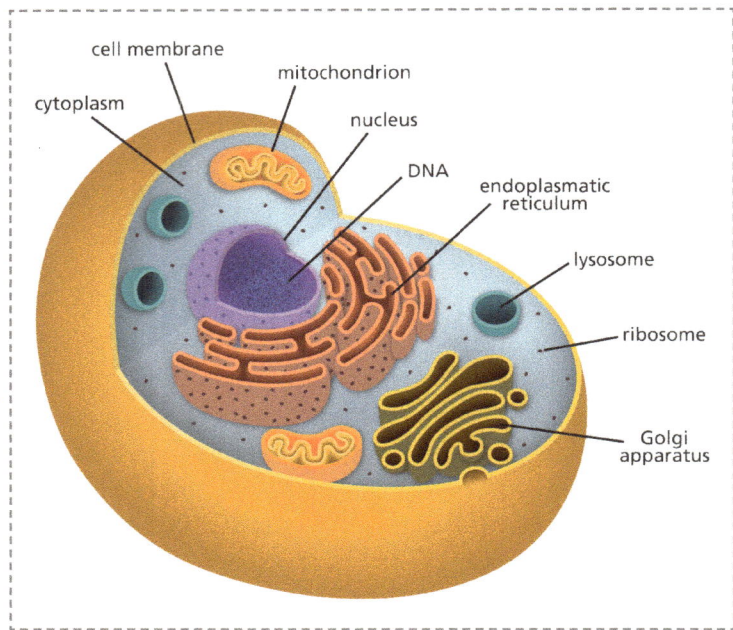

labels: cell membrane, mitochondrion, cytoplasm, nucleus, DNA, endoplasmatic reticulum, lysosome, ribosome, Golgi apparatus

The cell is an incredible marvelous organic factory of organelles and delivery systems that generate the tissues and organs that make up every living thing on earth. The order and intricacy of this building block of life prove the Creator's existence and His incredible ingenuity.[22]

1. Epithelial Cells. These cells are tightly attached to one another and cover the interior of hollow organs, like blood vessels, intestines, and ducts, or else they form the surface of things, like the skin. There are dozens of types of epithelial cells, without which there would be no skin to protect your body from injury or dehydration, and it would not be possible to digest food.

2. Nerve Cells. These cells are specialized for communication. They send signals from the brain to muscles and glands that control their functions. They also receive sensory information from the skin, the eyes, and the ears, and send this information to the brain. There are dozens of varieties of nerve cells in the body, each with individual shapes and functions which enable control over your bodily functions.

3. Muscle Cells. These cells are specialized for contraction, of which there are three kinds: cardiac, smooth, and skeletal. They contract and relax, pulling on bones and tendons to produce motion. They also form the thick outer walls of hollow organs like blood vessels and intestines, and contract or relax to regulate the diameter of these hollow organs.

4. Connective Tissue Cells. These cells provide structural strength to the body, and also defend against foreign invaders like bacteria. They come in two types: fibroblasts and fat cells. Other cells migrate into these connective tissues from the bloodstream to fight diseases. Special types of connective tissues — cartilage and bone — are designed for strength and rigidity to support the body and connect muscles to bones.

These various cells have been programmed since conception to specialize into the many organs that support the life of the body, and they in turn are deftly arranged into systems for cooperative effort. These twelve systems are as follows. Note that the number twelve signifies a perfect governmental foundation or completion[24] ... each of the twelve working together as a oneness, a unity of cooperation to produce the maximum health and longevity of the entire organism.[25]

1. Circulatory System. This system, consisting of the heart, blood, blood vessels, arteries, and veins, is designed to move blood, nutrients, oxygen, carbon dioxide, and hormones throughout the body. A single drop of blood contains 5,000,000 red blood cells, 10,000 white blood cells, and 250,000 platelets.[26] The total length of a single person's blood vessels would wrap around the earth two times. An average human heart will beat about 100,000 times a day, or around 3,000,000,000 times during a lifetime, sending red blood cells around the body in about 20 seconds.[27] The blood cells themselves are produced in the bone marrow. Not to be minimized is the importance of structured water along the inner surfaces of capillaries to help move blood through the capillaries, to cells, and back to the heart.[28]

2. Digestive System.[30] This series of connected organs allows the body to break down and absorb food, and remove waste. It begins with the mouth, where food is chewed and mixed with saliva, which begins

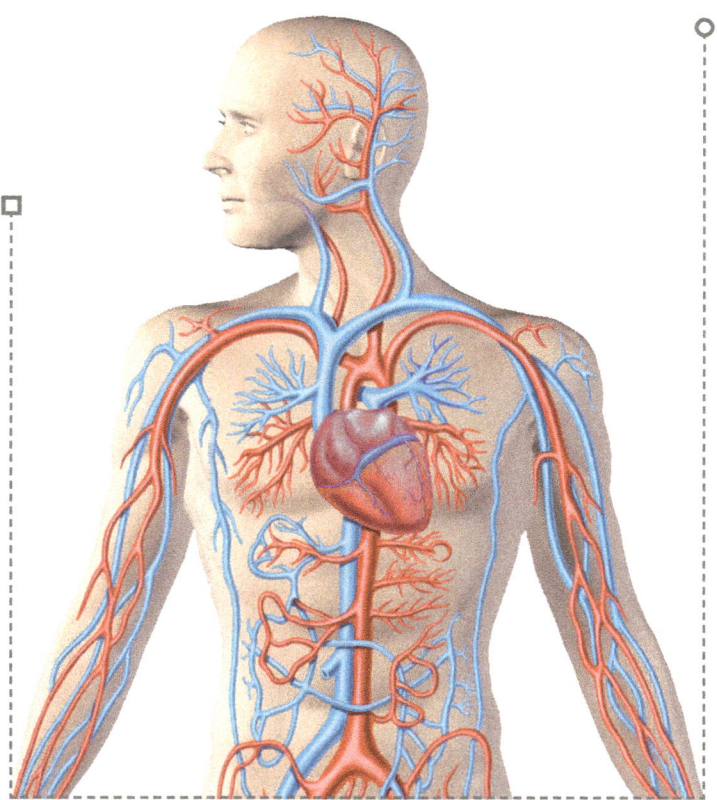

The human circulatory system is designed to move the blood throughout he body, to nourish and detoxify every single cell, thus making life possible. Truly the life is in the blood.[29]

the breakdown process, especially with amylase that converts starches into sugars. The tongue pushes food into your throat, and during swallowing the epiglottis folds over your windpipe to prevent choking, and the food passes into the esophagus. When food reaches the end of the esophagus, a ring-like muscle called the lower esophageal sphincter

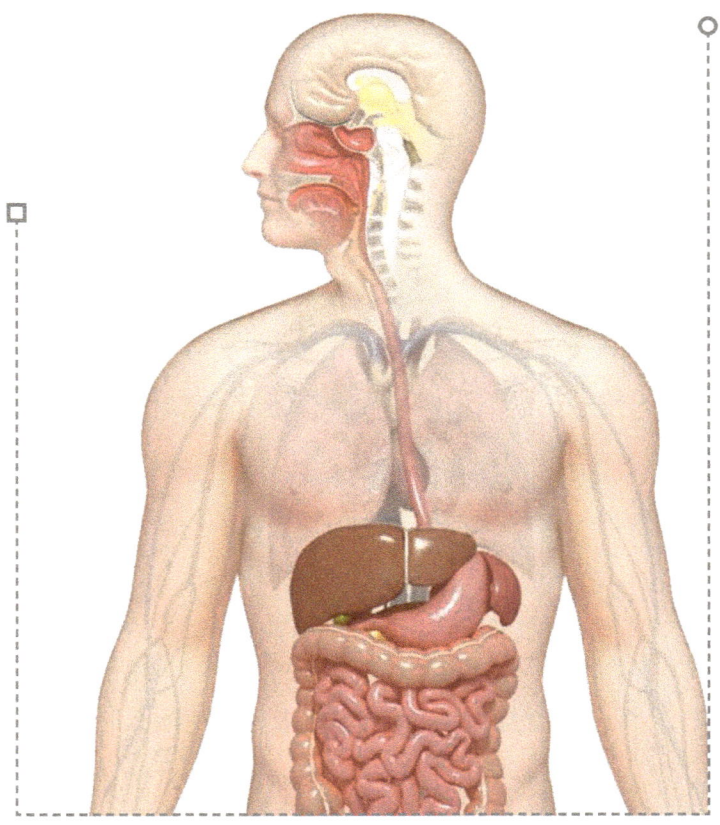

The digestive system of the human body takes foods produced by chlorophyll acting together with water, minerals, air, and sunlight, and converts them into useful compounds which provide energy and structure for living, which are distributed to every cell by the blood[33].

intestine. Muscles of the small intestine mix food with digestive juices from the pancreas, liver, and intestine, and push the mixture forward for further digestion. The walls of the small intestine absorb water and the digested nutrients into your bloodstream, and are aided in the breakdown of food products by an army of about 100 trillion bacteria, weighing about four pounds for the average adult.[31] Villi along the intestinal wall serve to absorb these nutrients and deliver them to blood capillaries. As peristalsis continues, the waste products of the digestive process move into the large intestine, where further microbial activity creates vitamins, and finally peristalsis moves the material into the rectum. This digestive process greatly aids immunity, accounting for perhaps 70 percent of total immune function.[32]

3. Endocrine and Exocrine System.[34] The endocrine system contains five major glands that secrete hormones into the bloodstream which transports them throughout the body, to perform a number of functions including growth, development, metabolism, mood, and reproduction. They include the adrenals, thyroid, hypothalamus, pineal, and the overall master gland, the pituitary. Each gland's output is controlled by a complex interplay of physiological and mental processes to produce

relaxes and lets food pass into your stomach. This sphincter usually stays closed to keep the stomach's contents from flowing back into the esophagus. In the stomach, muscles mix the food and liquid with digestive juices and slowly empty its contents into the small effects amongst all of the body's tissues, though some of their hormones are targeted to affect certain tissues, such as the thyroid affecting sweating. These hormones travel to different tissues and regulate various bodily functions, such as metabolism, growth, and sexual function. Some organs also contain endocrine tissue — the pancreas, kidneys, ovaries, and testes; the latter two produce the testosterone and estrogen and other hormones involved in sexual development. The exocrine glands — salivary glands, sweat glands, mammary glands, and sebaceous and lacrimal glands — produce substances that are released through ducts to the exterior of the body.

4. Immune System.[35] This is the body's defense against bacteria, viruses, and other pathogens that may be harmful. It includes the lymph nodes, the spleen, bone marrow, lymphocytes (including B-cells and T-cells), the thymus gland, and leukocytes, which are white blood cells. The immune system is spread throughout the body and involves many types of cells, organs, proteins, and tissues. Crucially, it can distinguish our own tissue from foreign tissue — self from non-self. Dead and faulty cells are also recognized and cleared away by the immune system. If the immune system encounters a pathogen, such as a bacterium, virus, or parasite, it mounts a so-called immune response. White blood cells (leucocytes) are stored in lymphoid organs, including the thymus, spleen, bone marrow, and lymph nodes. They circulate throughout the body in blood vessels and lymphatic vessels and are on constant patrol for pathogens. When they find a target, they begin to multiply and send signals to other cell types to do likewise. The two main types of leucocytes are phagocytes, which surround and absorb pathogens, and lymphocytes, that help the body remember previous invaders and recognize them if they come back to attack again.

5. Lymphatic System.[37] Lymph nodes, lymph ducts, and lymph vessels, which permeate all cells and organs, also play a major role in the body's defenses. This system's main job is to make and move lymph, a clear fluid that contains white blood cells, which helps the body fight infection. The lymphatic system also removes excess lymph fluid from bodily tissues and returns it to the blood. The lymphatic system consists of lymph vessels, ducts, nodes, and other tissues. Around two quarts of fluid leak from the cardiovascular system into body tissues every day, and the lymphatic system is the network of vessels that collects these clear fluids. The lymph vessels form a network of branches that reach most of the body's tissues, and work in a similar way to the blood vessels, returning fluid from tissues to the blood. Unlike blood, the lymphatic fluid is not pumped but squeezed through the vessels when we use our muscles. These lymphatic vessels have valves inside them to stop fluid

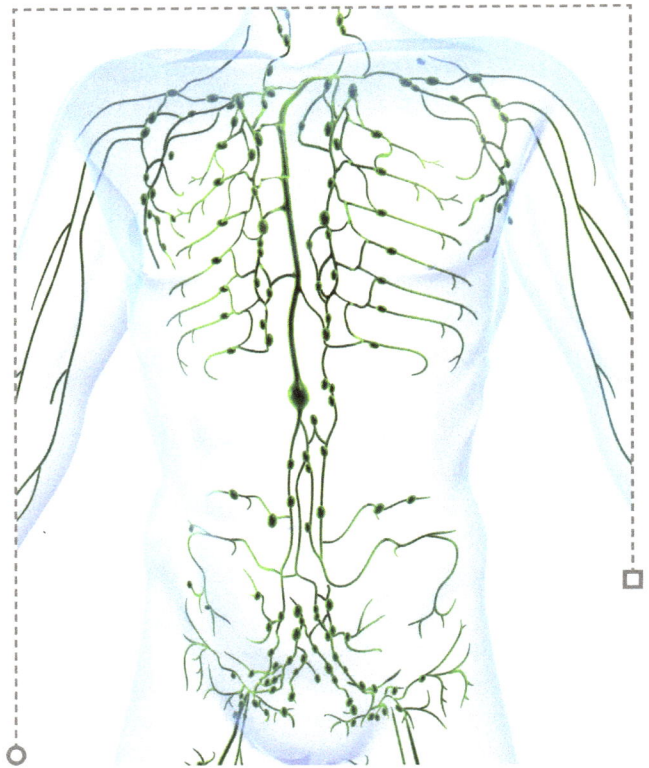

called lymph nodes. In the lymph nodes, immune cells examine the lymph for foreign material, such as bacteria, viruses, or fungi, and help remove them. Other lymphatic tissues in the body include the tonsils, spleen, and thymus gland.

6. Nervous System.[39] This marvelous system controls both voluntary action (conscious movement of skeletal muscles) and involuntary actions (such as breathing), and sends signals to different parts of the body. The system controls sensory, integrative, and motor functions throughout the body. The brain consists of the forebrain, midbrain, and hindbrain, with specific functions tied to various areas within these areas; it has over 100 trillion neural connections.[40] The central nervous system includes the brain, spinal cord, and ganglia. The peripheral nervous system consists of nerves that connect every other part of the body to the central nervous system. There are many types of specialized nerve cells,

The lymphatic system, a major part of the body's defenses and cleansing mechanisms, permeates the entire body, reaching every cell as does the blood of the circulatory system. It too typifies the love of our Creator by defending and purifying the body.[36]

from flowing back in the wrong direction. Lymph is drained progressively towards larger vessels until it reaches the two main channels, the lymphatic ducts in our trunk. From there, the filtered lymph fluid returns to the blood in the veins. The vessels branch through junctions

The brain, which serves as the control center of the nervous system, is an amazing organ that has the capacity to store about 2.5 million gigabytes of information, far more than any creation of man can generate. It serves in many respects as an interface of communication between God and man.[38]

containing dendrites and axons, for the eyes, ears, tongue, and other body parts to detect messages of pain, heat, cold, pressure, taste (salt, bitter, sweet), and the nuances of hearing, interpreting sounds, and interpreting and then expressing speech, as well as detecting colors and other details of sight.

7. Muscular System.[41] There are about 650 muscles throughout the body that aid in movement, blood flow, and other bodily functions. Three types of muscle are found:

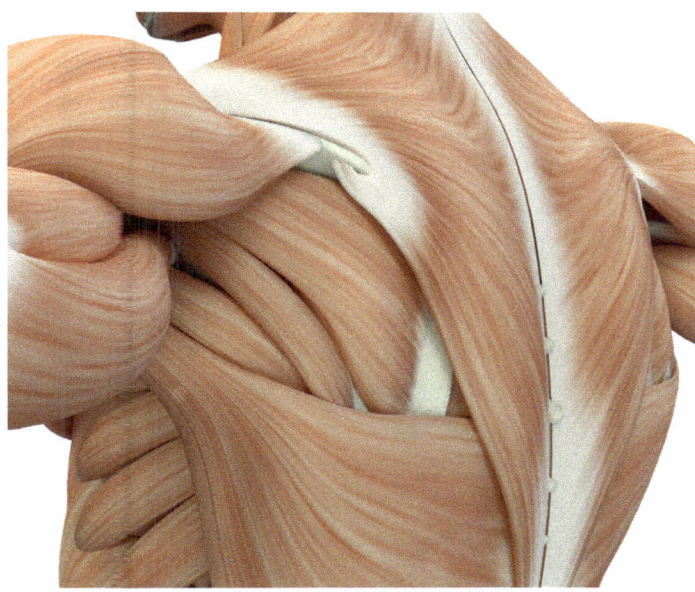

Muscles of the human body enable it to function and carry out the acts of service that is designed to accomplish … acts of love and kindness, peace and joy that make life what it ought to be, if lived in accordance with the Creator.[43]

skeletal muscle which is connected to bone and enables voluntary movement, smooth muscle which is found inside organs and helps move substances through organs, and cardiac muscle which is found in the heart and pumps blood. The heart is the hardest-working muscle, which pumps 2 ounces of blood with every heartbeat. Daily, the heart pumps at least 2,500 gallons (9,464 liters) of blood. The heart has the ability to beat more than 3 billion times in a person's life.[42] The main functions of the muscular system are to enable mobility, provide overall body stability, maintain posture, control circulation (contracting or relaxing around arteries), enable respiration (the diaphragm), move food along the intestines and stomach during digestion, enable urination, and move the child out of the uterus during childbirth.

8. Reproductive System.[44] Without this system the human race could not continue and would have been terminated after Adam and Eve's deaths. The male reproductive system includes the penis and the testes, which produce sperm, and associated ducts and glands. The female reproductive system consists of the vagina, uterus, fallopian tubes, and ovaries, which produce eggs. During conception, a sperm cell fuses with an egg cell, which creates a fertilized egg that implants and grows in the uterus.

9. Skeletal System.[45] Infants are born with about 300 separate bones, and as a child grows some of those bones fuse together until growth stops, typically by the age of 25, leaving the skeleton with 206 bones. Our bones are separated into two categories based on the purpose and location of the bones: the axial skeleton and the appendicular skeleton. The axial skeleton contains 80 bones, including the skull, spine, and rib cage, which form the central structure of the skeleton, with the function of protecting the brain, spinal cord, heart and lungs. The remaining 126 bones make up the appendicular skeleton, and include the arms, legs, shoulder girdle and pelvic girdle. The lower portion of the appendicular skeleton protects the major organs associated with digestion and reproduction and provides stability when a person is walking or running. The upper portion allows for a greater range of motion when lifting and carrying objects. The bones are connected by tendons, ligaments, and cartilage. The skeleton not only enables us to move, but is also involved in the production of blood cells in the marrow, and in the storage and releasing of calcium, phosphorus, and other minerals, as well as fats. The teeth are also part of the skeletal system, but are not considered to be bones.

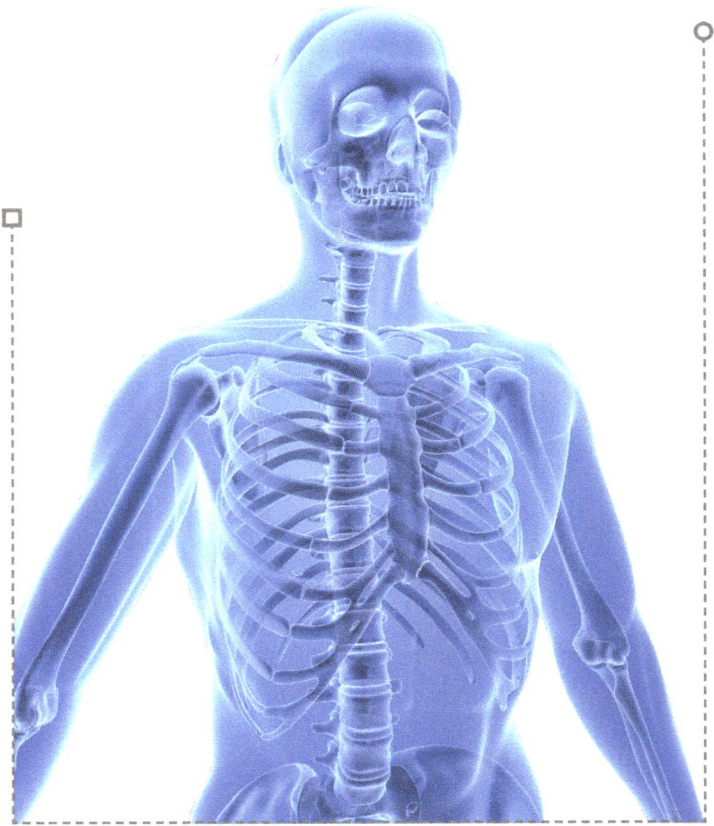

A skeletal system forms the rigid structure that enables the body to move, to function in the way that the Eternal designed as a vibrant servant, created to love his Creator and his fellow man.[46]

10. Respiratory System.[47] This marvelous system allows us to take in vital oxygen and expel carbon dioxide in a process we call breathing. It consists mainly of the trachea, the diaphragm, and the lungs. As we breathe, oxygen enters the nose or mouth and passes the sinuses, which are hollow spaces in the skull that help regulate the temperature

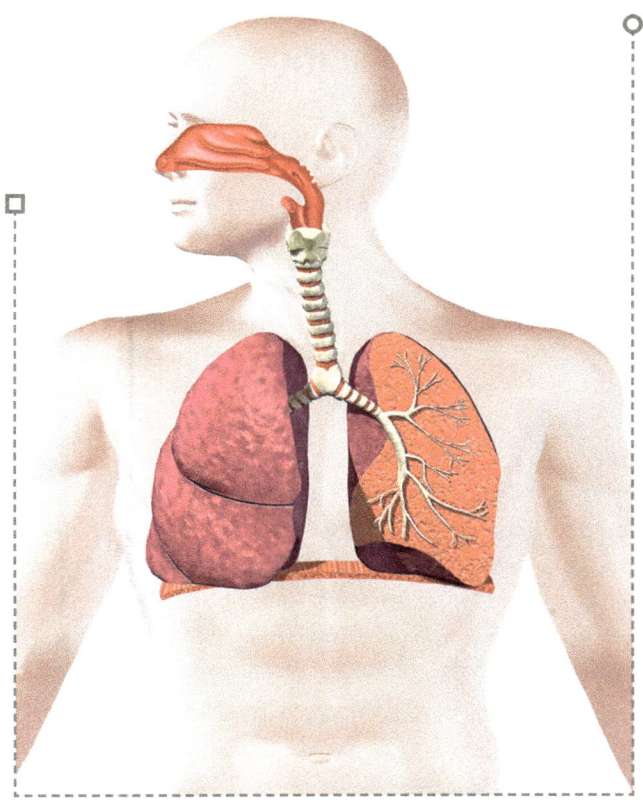

Without the exchange of air into the body the processes of cell respiration could not occur. The sinuses, trachea, and lungs bring in oxygen and expel carbon dioxide, enabling the transfer of gases to reach every cell in the body through the blood. Thus, air functions much like spirit.[48]

and humidity of the air we breathe. From the sinuses, air passes through the trachea, also called the windpipe, and into the bronchial tubes, which are the two tubes that carry air into each lung. The bronchial tubes are lined with tiny hairs called cilia that move back and forth, carrying mucus up and out. Mucus is a sticky fluid that collects dust, germs, and other matter that has invaded the lungs and is expelled by sneezing and coughing. The bronchial tubes split up again to carry air into the lobes of each lung. The right lung has three lobes while the left lung has only two, to accommodate room for the heart. The lobes are filled with small, spongy sacs called alveoli where the exchange of oxygen and carbon dioxide occurs. The alveolar walls are extremely thin (about 0.2 micrometers) and are composed of a single layer of tissues called epithelial cells, and tiny blood vessels called pulmonary capillaries. Blood in the capillaries picks up oxygen and drops off carbon dioxide. The oxygenated blood then makes its way to the pulmonary vein. This vein carries oxygen-rich blood to the left side of the heart, where it is pumped to all parts of the body. The carbon dioxide the blood left behind moves into the alveoli and gets expelled in our exhaled breath.

11. Urinary System.[49] This system helps eliminate a waste product called urea from the body, which is produced when certain foods are broken down. The whole system includes two kidneys, two ureters, the bladder, two sphincter muscles, and the urethra. Urine produced by the kidneys travels down the ureters to the bladder, and exits the body through the urethra. The urinary system works with the lungs, skin, and intestines to maintain the balance of chemicals and water in the body.

Adults eliminate about 27 to 68 fluid ounces per day. Other factors in urinary system function include fluid lost through perspiring and breathing. The primary organs of the urinary system are the kidneys, which are bean-shaped organs that are located just below the rib cage in the middle of the back. The kidneys remove urea, a waste compound formed by the breakdown of proteins, from the blood through small filtering units called nephrons. Each nephron consists of a ball formed of small blood capillaries, called a glomerulus, and a small tube called a renal tubule. Urea, together with water and other waste substances, forms the urine as it passes through the nephrons and down the renal tubules of the kidney. From the kidneys, urine travels down two thin tubes, called ureters, to the bladder.

12. The Skin, or Integumentary System.[50]
The skin is the body's largest organ. It acts as a protective barrier between the outside and the inside of the body, and is our first defense against bacteria, viruses, and other pathogens. Our skin also helps regulate body temperature and eliminate waste through perspiration. In addition to skin, the integumentary system includes hair and nails. In adults, skin accounts for about 14 percent of total body weight and covers a surface area of approximately 22 square feet. There are different thicknesses and textures of skin on different parts of the body, such as skin that is paper-thin underneath the eyes, but is thick on the soles of the feet and palms of the hand. Human skin is composed of three layers of tissue: epidermis, dermis, and hypodermis. The epidermis is the top, visible layer of skin and is constantly being renewed as dead skin cells are shed on a daily basis. The main functions of the epidermis include making new skin cells, giving skin its color, and protecting the skin. The dermis is the middle layer of skin, found underneath the epidermis. It is the thickest layer of skin and contains nerves and blood vessels. It is also home to the sweat glands, oil glands, and hair follicles. The dermis gives skin its flexibility and strength. It is made up mostly of a protein called collagen that makes skin stretchy and strong. The dermis is important for sensing pain and touch, producing sweat and oils, growing hair, bringing blood to the skin, and fighting infection. The hypodermis (subcutaneous fat) is the deepest layer of skin that helps insulate the body from heat and cold. It serves as an energy storage area for fat, which additionally provides padding to cushion internal organs as well as muscles and bones, and protects the body from injuries.

The above brief descriptions of the structure and functions of the human body do not do justice to the incredible intricacies and wonderment of this fabulously designed biological/chemical/electrical/spiritual organism. The human body is a marvelous creation in God's own image. It is the very image of the Creator Himself, with the organs and systems that He has in spirit. The better we can understand the body — its parts and functions and interactions — the better we can understand the Eternal Himself, since each of these parts and what it does has symbolic meaning. Throughout Scripture the heart, the bowels, the belly (intestines), the ears, the eyes, and other body parts are mentioned in various contexts. Even the nervous system is referred to in many cases, directly or indirectly, especially regarding pain and suffering, but also with references to joy and love.

Love! There is that word again, and it is the essence of the makeup of the wonderful body that the Creator made in His express image. It is an image of unimaginable cooperation and serving of each part with the other parts. One cannot separate the parts from one another, since they all serve important functions for the life and longevity of the entire organism. Some are more important than others in the sense that the body cannot live long without them: the liver, heart, lungs, brain, intestines, pancreas, kidneys, bladder, and bones. Some we can live without — the spleen, appendix, tonsils, parts of the intestines and stomach, toes, and even entire legs and arms. Even then other parts of the body strive valiantly to make up for the loss so the body can continue on, albeit perhaps at a slower, less efficient pace. Yet, it will continue on as best it can, for life is so precious. This process is called *accommodation*: the body as a whole adjusts the functions of its tissues and organs for the greatest longevity, extending life to the greatest possible limits.[51]

We are reminded of I Corinthians 12, where each member of the ecclesia is likened to a part of the body.

"For as the body is one and has many members, but all the members of that one body, being many, but one body, so also is Christ…. For in fact the body is not one member but many…. But now God has set the members, each one of them, in the body as He pleased. And if they were all one member, where would the body be? But now indeed there are many members, yet one body…. But our presentable parts have no need. But God composed the body, having given greater honor to that part which lacks it, that there should be no schism in the body, but that the members should have the same care for one another. And if one member suffers, all the members suffer with it; or if one member is honored, all the members rejoice with it. Now you are the body of Christ, and members individually" (I Corinthians 12:12, 14, 18-20, 24-27).

I have shown just a few examples within the plant, animal, microbial, and human realms of how the concept of love is operating continually, before our very eyes! Indeed, "Love makes the world go 'round." It is selfless giving by one party to benefit another that allows our world to prosper and be in health. The beauty of this mutualism is that everyone wins. A direct consequence of doing good to others is that good will come back to you. As Christ said in Luke 6:38,

> "Give and it will be given to you; good measure, pressed down, shaken together, and running over will be put into your bosom. For with the same measure that you use, it will be measured back to you."

What better definition of mutualism can there be than that? This message runs all through the created world. True to the message of Paul that "… His invisible attributes are clearly seen, being understood by the things that are made …" (Romans 1:20), love permeates the entire created world. We just need to look, see, and believe. It is clearly displayed as evidence of the Maker's handiwork!

Moreover, the very covenants that Yahweh made with Abraham and Israel imply this mutualism that we see throughout the creation. A covenant can be described as "two parties working together to produce greater results than either of them working alone."[52] This is the very definition of mutualism, a type of symbiosis found throughout the natural world and as revealed in this chapter. Thus, the covenants that have been agreed upon between our great God, and each of us who has been called out of this world of sin, are expressions of the love the Eternal has for us, a love that goes deeper than any of us can possibly imagine!

Thus, the covenants that have been agreed upon between our great God, and each of us who has been called out of this world of sin, are expressions of the love the Eternal has for us, a love that goes deeper than any of us can possibly imagine!

Cooperation and kindness are the hallmarks of a properly ordered relationship, be it within the ecosphere or in the sphere of human relationships.[53]

Life is hardly worth living without good health, and the eternal God so generously showers us with exuberant health because of His love for us, that we might be lively servants of Him and our fellow man.[1]

THE NINTH BRANCH

LOVE IS THE GRANTING OF HEALTH & FULFILLMENT

She was prim and proper. The once barren room was filled with artwork and photographs. Pictures and memories. You could barely tell that she was in essence living in a nursing home. The food was better. The nurses and aids maybe slightly more solicitous. But underneath the sheen, her daily activities were supervised by a team of medical professionals dedicated to the small number of wealthy people who had the cash to buy into this elite retirement community. She dwelled most of the last decade in the independent wing. After her husband's death, she moved to the assisted living side. And now after her recent hospitalization and the masses were seen on a cat scan, she landed in the skilled services area. Despite all attempts at clinging to that which had made her happy over the years, she was flailing miserably. No matter how hard she tried, money couldn't buy health.

And boy did she try.

Although death was staring her in the face, her basic coping mechanism was to pretend that nothing had changed. The rich baroness that she was, nothing made her more happy than ordering people around. She scolded the certified nursing assistant for not arranging her food tray just so. She manhandled the nurse when her meds were a few minutes late. Each verbal lashing accompanied by the same refrain: "I didn't pay all this money to be treated so!"

Money … the weapon she tossed around like a dagger slicing through all who chose to come near. She replaced her regular doctor, and paid a few thousand dollars extra to have a concierge one. Although money can't buy health, it can grant access. Her dollars paid for late night calls and much hand-holding. It paid for her obnoxious behavior and snooty ways.

Second opinions were forthcoming. Not only medical but intellectual and spiritual. She was visited daily by an array of advisors. Religious, alternative medicine, and just about every kook she could wave a hundred-dollar bill at. She proclaimed the rightness of any who would deny that her fate was sealed. She argued relentlessly with her medical team based on her astrologer's recommendations.

Her vigor and incivility were notorious. Money can't buy health, but it can excuse inexcusable behavior.

She was tolerated because of her net worth. Otherwise she would have been thrown to the curb.

There was no shortage of family members tromping in and out of her room. They came in with solicitous smiles and honeyed tongues. They tolerated every last cruel and insensitive opinion that she bowled their way. She held the inheritance

Sunshine, fresh air, excellent diet, plenty of exercise, and a positive outlook on life … all of these things conspire to grant wonderful health and vitality to individuals and families, and allow love to flow amidst the rigors of living within an age of chaos.[4]

above each like a tiny gold-plated carrot atop a very long stick. They jumped and jumped to try to grasp the treasure. Money can't buy health, but her progeny definitely saw it as an easy route to happiness … a happiness in which they could use their wealth to treat people just as poorly.

They would fight for her favor. Fight from her very first breath each day to her very last.

Her vile behavior lasted until the very end. She wheeled her material wealth like a battle-axe aiming to cripple the illness which had taken over her body. But the masses progressed. And her battle-axe did more self-harm than anything else. She sent all the staff, family, and friends fleeing away as opposed to huddling by her side.

There was no sadness when she passed. Money can't buy health. It can't buy meaning. There is no way to pay your way to being loved.

It can buy, however, fear and disgust. Relief. A staff of dedicated healthcare workers no longer suffering the abuse … and a gaggle of family members fighting among themselves and licking their chops at the spoils of an inheritance … so that they could live equally miserable lives and die equally tragic deaths …
Alone.[2]

I have no idea if this wealthy baroness was an actual person or just the character in a tragic story, but the message the story portrays is true to life, and has been played out countless times throughout history. Money cannot buy health, but in fact the love of it is the root of all evil (I Timothy 6:10). That evil includes disease and heartache, a life replete with material things but short on true fulfillment, love, and friends. Jesus knew this so very well.

"I have come that they may have life, and that they may have it more abundantly" (John 10:10).
abundantly = *perissos*, "what is above and over, superadded, hence what is superior and advantageous."[2]

What a statement! Jesus Christ came not that we might have a mundane, uneventful, drab, useless, and unhealthy life that depended on an abundance of physical possessions. He came that we might find joy, peace, love, true happiness, and exuberant health and energy! That is the life Jesus had …not forgetting that in this world He, like us, was tempted in all ways as we are (Hebrews 4:15), and suffered greatly at times just like we do. In fact, we must suffer or we will not enter the kingdom of heaven (Romans 8:17). Jesus Himself was prophesied to endure much grief on earth.

"He is despised and rejected by men, a man of sorrow and acquainted with grief. And we hid, as it were, our faces from Him; He was despised, and we did not esteem Him. Surely He has borne our griefs and carried our sorrows: yet we esteemed Him stricken, smitten by God, and afflicted. But He was wounded for our transgressions, He was

"*I have come that they may have life, and that they may have it more abundantly*" (John 10:10).

bruised for our iniquities; the chastisement for our peace was upon Him, and by His stripes we are healed" (Isaiah 53:3-5).

The desire of Jesus that we might live an abundant life was seconded by the Apostle John when he said,

"Beloved, I pray that you may prosper in all things and be in health, just as your soul prospers" (III John 2).
prosper = euodoo, "to help on the road, succeed in reaching."[5]
health = hugiaino, "to have sound health, be well (in body)."[6]

There can be few ways our eternal Creator could have granted us to display His great love for us than to provide good health … health of body, mind, and spirit. He shows us that good health is the result of following the commandments and laws He has given us as a safeguard.

"If you diligently heed the voice of the Lord your God and do what is right in His sight, give ear to His commandments and keep all His statutes, I will put none of the diseases on you which I have brought on the Egyptians. For I am the Lord who heals you" (Exodus 15:26).

The Diseases of Egypt

The Egyptians suffered certain horrible diseases and maladies as a result of their not following the diet and lifestyle of the Creator, but what were they? These diseases are mentioned in Deuteronomy 7:15, 28:27, and 28:60, especially in Deuteronomy 28:27.

"The Lord will strike you with the boils of Egypt, with tumors, with the scab, and with the itch, from which you cannot be healed" (NKJV).

Four maladies are mentioned here: boils, tumors, scab, and itch. Let us take a brief look at these illnesses that were endemic among the Egyptian people.

Boils = Hebrew *shechiyn*, "an inflamed ulcer, a boil."[7] The word is translated *botch* in the KJV, and according to some scholars may refer to a "black leprosy," or elephantiasis, where the feet and legs swell and the skin becomes black and scaly. The word is translated botch in Deuteronomy 28:27 and 35, but

Job suffered through the agonies of painful boils, from head to foot, but through the trial learned the lessons he needed to grow in love toward his Creator and his family. Such trials produce the fruits of righteousness.[11]

translated boil everywhere else in the KJV (Exodus 9:9-11; Leviticus 13:18-23; II Kings 20:7; Job 2:7; Isaiah 38:21). Boils seem to be the most likely candidate for this aliment, since Deuteronomy 28:35 refers to these outbreaks occurring "from the sole of your foot to the top of your head," reminiscent of Job's boils that gave him misery for months on end, so painful that he preferred death over life (Job 2:7; 3). It was the grievous affliction granted the Egyptians during the sixth plague.

Tumors = Hebrew *tchor*, "to burn, a boil or ulcer (from the inflammation), especially piles."[8] The KJV translates this word *emerods*, as it does in I Samuel 5:6, 9, 12 and 6:4, 5, 11, and 17. The Hebrew root gives the idea of a swelling or mound, and is used for "tower" in II Kings 5:24, and "fort" in Isaiah 32:14. "Tumor" fits this idea quite well. If hemorrhoids are implied here, then a very uncomfortable ailment is described.

Scab = Hebrew *cappachath*," the mange (as making the hair fall off)."[9] Mange is a skin disorder caused by a parasitic mite that invades the skin and causes severe itching. This aliment is mentioned in Leviticus 13:2, 6-8; 14:56; 21:20; 22:22; Deuteronomy 28:27; and Isaiah 3:17

Itch = Hebrew *cherec*, " to scrape; the itch."[10] It is mentioned only in Deuteronomy 28:27, immediately after scab, so may be related closely to it in the sense of causing severe skin irritation.

Eating Unclean Foods

These are only some of the diseases the Egyptians could expect to experience, since they ate unclean foods and engaged in devious sexual and other practices that also lead to various ailments. Let us look at the afflictions that can arise from eating unclean foods such as pigs, horses, rats, shellfish, and crustaceans.

Hepatitis.[12] Eating pork and certain other

Certain foods give rise to diseases in man which our Creator intended that we avoid. We need to heed His instructions and reap the fruits of abundant living by conforming to the laws of health revealed to us.[18]

unclean meats leads to a much higher incidence of Hepatitis E, especially when the much-desired liver is consumed. In today's developed nations, pork liver is the top food-based transmitter of this disease that can cause fever, fatigue, jaundice, vomiting, joint pain, other pains, liver failure, and death. A whopping 20 million people each year contract this illness, and it would be naive to assume that ancient societies such as Egypt also did not experience it. Up to 40 percent of U.S. hogs test positive for Hepatitis E.

Multiple sclerosis (MS).[13] There is a close relationship between pork consumption and MS, the myelin-attacking autoimmune condition which affects the central nervous system. In countries such as Germany and Denmark, where pork is consumed liberally, the pork intake versus MS correlation is nearly perfect (0.87), whereas the beef intake to MS correlation shows no relationship. It has been found that some pork slaughter plant workers developed MS-like symptoms after inhaling "pig brain mist" created by pig brain tissue blasted into the air during processing. The workers' immune systems formed antibodies to the foreign porcine antigens, which closely resemble myelin proteins surrounding and protecting their nerves. Then the workers' own immune systems began attacking the myelin, causing MS. To suggest that the Egyptians did not suffer from autoimmune disease identical or similar to MS, due to eating unclean meats, is being disingenuous.

Liver cancer and cirrhosis.[14] While liver problems are closely related to hepatitis B and C infection, aflatoxin exposure, and excessive alcohol intake, pork consumption also shows a very high correlation to liver cancer and cirrhosis. Beef, on the other hand, has shown protective effects on the liver. The liver-pork connection may be due to the typical use of nitrates and nitrites as curing agents for bacon and ham, which leads to cancer-causing nitrosamine formation. It is not known if the Egyptians used curing agents for their meats, but they could have.

Yersinia.[15] Eating uncooked or undercooked pork can lead to yersiniosis, caused by Yersinia bacteria which produce fever, pain, and bloody diarrhea. The long-term consequences are much more serious: various types of arthritis, in particular reactive arthritis, a type of inflammatory joint disease that is 47 times higher in Yersinia victims, and other diseases such as liver abscesses, eye problems, and Grave's disease. The Egyptians may have eaten undercooked pork and other unclean animals, leading to these maladies.

Trichinosis.[16] Trichina worms have been prevalent in pigs, bears, and certain other unclean animals, more so in hogs in years past than today, but a significant percentage of hogs still harbor the worms in their muscle tissues. Symptoms of trichinosis include nausea, vomiting, diarrhea, fatigue, fever, and abdominal pain, which can graduate to headaches, joint pain, coughing, eye swelling, and constipation The trichina worms travel to muscles in the body where they create cysts, and can remain there for years. The Egyptians most certainly experienced some trichinosis, as have many pork eaters throughout the past centuries, since it was a common ailment.

Worm infestation.[17] Roundworms (such as Trichina worms, mentioned above), pinworms, hookworms, and tapeworms can be contracted by eating pork and most unclean animals. While cooking kills these worms, not everyone in Egypt or the Old World likely understood this need for heating meat to rid it of worm eggs. As a result, the insults of internal parasites plagued ancient societies, as they do many modern cultures who avoid cooking meat thoroughly, or who eat unclean animals.

Bacterial infections.[19] Pork and other unclean meats can harbor several pathogenic organisms, including *Salmonella*, *Escherichia coli*, *Listeria monocytogenes*, and *Staphylococcus aureus*. These microbes existed in Egypt, as they do worldwide today. Though cooking will kill most of them, the *Staphylococcus aureus* toxins are not deactivated by heat and cause acute food poisoning and the usual nausea, vomiting, and diarrhea associated with tainted unclean meats.

Vibriosis.[120] A bacteria in warm, saltwater, coastal environments infects oysters and clams which, when eaten raw or undercooked,

Leprosy is but one of many curses that can afflict people. With this disease, and every other illness, we can go to the great Healer and be cured through our faith in Him, if it is indeed His will that we be healed.[23]

leads to watery diarrhea, stomach cramps, vomiting, fever, and chills. The Egyptians most certainly consumed unclean creatures from the Nile River and Mediterranean coastal waters.

Other seafood-transmitted microbes.[21] Shellfish, lobsters, shrimp, and other unclean creatures in ocean or lake environments filter the water and accumulate whatever microbes are present. Some are pathogenic, including vibrio species — as shown above — *Salmonella*, *Shigella* species, *Clostridium botulinum*, *Staphylococcus* species, *Norovirus*, Hepatitis A virus, helminths (worms), and protozoa such as Giardia and amoebas. Whether cooked or not, the residents of Egypt most certainly partook of many unclean creatures from the waters around them, in particular the many Nile Delta tributaries, and suffered from the discomforts of food-borne illnesses.

Another major disease of Egypt was *leprosy* (Hebrew *tsaraath*).[22] It is mentioned in Leviticus 13 and 14 and Deuteronomy 24:8,

and was a particularly nasty, contagious disease that required careful quarantine of victims. The causative organism could even infect walls of homes and be transmitted by household objects and clothing. This ailment has been plaguing civilization throughout recorded history, in China, Egypt, India, and the Middle East. The modern term for it is Hanson's Disease, caused by the *Mycobacterium leprae* bacteria, though there is some questions as to whether the ancient leprosy is exactly the same as the modern version. Not particularly contagious, it nevertheless affects the peripheral nerves and causes disfiguring skin sores, lumps, and bumps that remain after weeks or months. Skin sores are pale-colored. Victims lose feeling in their arms and legs, and muscles become weak. Because there is a loss of feeling, lepers will injure their affected parts without realizing the damage. The symptoms usually take 3 to 5 years to appear after initial infection, but may take as long as 20 years. The manifestation of the disease is either tuberculoid (only one or a few patches of flat, pale-colored skin that feels numb) or lepromatous (widespread skin bumps, rashes, numbness, and muscle weakness, and nose, kidney, and male reproductive organ involvement), or somewhere between. Having come out of Egypt, the Israelites were carefully instructed in dealing with this insidious disease for the purpose of eradicating it from the nation.

Sexual Deviancy and Disease

Besides the ailments arising from unclean and microbe-contaminated foods, or infectious diseases transmitted by contact with disease carriers, there were sexually transmitted diseases the Egyptians had to contend with. The Egyptian people were, like the Canaanites, noted for sexual deviancy, which Israel was warned to avoid lest the "... land vomits out its inhabitants" (Leviticus 18:25; 20:10-21). These aberrations included incest, adultery, homosexuality, and bestiality (Leviticus 18). Moreover, prostitution (Leviticus 19:29) and ceremonial prostitution to idols (Leviticus 20:5-6) were not uncommon, and were forbidden for Israel.

"You shall therefore keep all My statutes and all My judgments, and perform them, that the land where I am bringing you to dwell may not vomit you out. And you shall not walk in the statutes of the nations which I am casting out before you; for they commit all these things, and therefore I abhor them" (Leviticus 20:22-23).

What are the diseases that can be passed on through illicit sexual activities? We call these "sexually transmitted diseases" (STDs).[24]

Chlamydia. Caused by the bacterium *Chlamydia trachomatis*, this disease leads to discharges, pain, urinary tract and pelvic inflammation, pregnancy problems, and infertility.

Herpes. The *Herpes simplex* virus produces blisters, headaches, backaches, itching, skin lesions, and pain.

Human papilloma virus (HPV). This common STD can cause cervical cancer and other skin manifestations.

Gonorrhea. The bacterium causes swelling, discharge, pain, and other symptoms.

Syphilis. A spirochete (*Treponema pallidum*) causes this STD, which will attack any organ in the body and, if left untreated, will kill, maim, or cause insanity.

Trichonomiasis. This protozoan disease can cause a wide array of symptoms, including infertility.

AIDS. Acquired Immune Deficiency Syndrome is caused by a virus which is normally innocuous. However, when recreational or other drugs are used by homosexuals and certain others, thus inhibiting immune function, the virus can multiply and further damage the body's immune system, especially CD4 cells (white blood cells). This leads to infections like pneumonia that the body would normally fight off, but cannot due to suppressed immunity.

Several of these STDs — and others too numerous to list here — were most certainly spread throughout Egyptian society, just as they were within the immoral Canaanite tribes. The laws of God prohibited Israel from partaking of the evil behavior that would precipitate these STDs.

Avoiding These Diseases

Now we have a fairly good grasp of the diseases of the Egyptians, which the Eternal said he would not lay upon Israel if they would "... give ear to His commandments and keep all His statutes" (Exodus 15:26). That begs the question, how does keeping God's commands and statutes keep a person from acquiring any of these hideous diseases? After all, it is the normal state of humankind to be healthy.

We must understand first of all that God never causes illness. He is the Author of exuberant and endless health, even as Jesus stated, "I have come that they may have life, and that they may have it more abundantly" (John 10:10). Notice that this statement follows His declaration that, "The thief does not come except to steal, and to kill, and to destroy" (John 10:10). Jesus Christ is the great Healer, the One who removed the afflictions of countless people during His time on the earth (Matthew 4:23-24; 9:35; 10:1-8; Mark 1:29-34; Luke 8:49-56; etc.), and who commissioned His disciples to do likewise (Matthew 10:10; Luke 9:1; Mark 16:18).

This tells us that the author of death, illness (the precursor to death), and destruction is the one who is a thief, obviously an allusion to Satan, the great law-breaker from the beginning. We know from numerous examples that Satan and his minions are the instigators of disease and death, such as the affliction of Job with boils (Job 2:7), the killing of the firstborn of Egypt by the death angel (Exodus 12:12-13), and the killing of many in

Israel from an angel sent by Yahweh due to David's sin of numbering Israel (I Chronicles 21:9-15). While Job 42:11 states that the misfortunes Job had to endure were approved by Yahweh, we know from Job 2:7 that it was Satan who did the "dirty work" and actually caused the afflictions.

Recall that the *serpent* (*nachash*, or Satan)[26] in Genesis 3:17-19 tempted Adam and Eve to sin, which brought on aging and death, not only to them but to the entire human race thereafter. We also have records of certain individuals throughout the centuries — including during the time that Jesus walked the earth — who have been afflicted by diseases caused by evil spirits (Luke 13:16). Note the following scriptures that show Satan is the instigator of sickness: Matthew 4:24; 12:22-28; Mark 9:25; Luke 7:21-22; 8:1-2; 13:11-16; Acts 10:38;

19:11-12; I Corinthians 5:1-5; Hebrews 2:14.

It is not the Eternal Creator who afflicts. Rather, He commissions spirits to carry out His work for specific purposes to fulfill His plan.

The Function of the Law

God's laws and statutes define sin, for "... sin is the transgression of the law" (I John 3:4; see also Romans 4:15 and I John 5:17). For Exodus 15:26 to be true, which states that if a person keeps God's commandments and statutes he will not get the diseases of Egypt, then there has to be a connection between the laws of God and illness. Let us take a look at the commandments of God as they relate to the prevention of disease. Recall that breaking one commandment breaks all ten (James 2:10).

Commandment 1. "You shall have no other gods before Me" (Exodus 20:3). Placing some other spiritual entity before the one true living God leaves a person open to following whatever moral code he desires. This is humanism at its core, making god in Your own image. By doing so, the perfect instructions that protect one's health will be voided.

With sin and the eventual expulsion from the Garden of Eden, death and suffering multiplied as families strove to gain their existence through sweat and hard labor. With aging came sickness and pain outside the Garden.[25]

Commandment 2. "You shall not make for yourself a carved image .... You shall not bow down to them nor serve them" (Exodus 20:4-6). Closely tied to Commandment 1, worshipping idols is essentially worshipping the demonic entities the makers of these images believed inhabited the idols. Such faith in evil spirits cannot lead to health and longevity, as Adam and Eve sadly learned. Such idol worship is a renunciation of the Source of all good reserved for a full, abundant, healthful life, who created mankind to be in excellent health and live forever if people would but follow His commands.

Getting adequate rest is no small matter, and for that reason man was given the command to rest from his labors on the seventh day, as well as get adequate rest every other day of the week.[29]

Commandment 3. "You shall not take the name of the Lord your God in vain ..." (Exodus 20:7). The Hebrew for *vain* is *lassaw*, meaning "worthlessness, vanity, falseness."[27] This commandment means much more than cursing by using His Name improperly, but it means denying His power: who He is and what He has done as Creator, and what He will do as the fulfiller of prophesies and prayers. To deny His omnipotence and the truth that He is our Creator and Sustainer — as do evolutionists and atheists — is to take the name of God in vain. It is the denial of God as the giver of life and health, the denial of His ability to heal our every disease (Psalm 103:3; 147:3; Jeremiah 17:14; James 5:14-15).

Commandment 4. "Remember the Sabbath day, to keep it holy. Six days you shall labor and do all your work, but the seventh day is the Sabbath of the Lord your God. In it you shall do no work ..." (Exodus 20:8-10). Weekly rest is essential to human kind's well-being. Such is not the case for spirits (Psalm 121:4), but people in their sinful fleshly nature require a certain amount of it. Without adequate sleep of at least seven hours a day, most people's immune systems grow weaker, and they fall prey to diseases. A severe lack of rest leads to psychotic abnormalities.[28]

Commandment 5. "Honor your father and your mother ..." (Exodus 20:12). This commandment carries with it the promise of long life, a direct reflection of good relationships with one's parents that reduce anxiety and stress throughout life. In fact, mental stress is perhaps the major cause of illness in the world, a fact attested to by S.I. McMillan in his book *None of These Diseases*.[30] As a medical doctor, he estimated that 80% or more of hospital beds were occupied by people suffering from anger, frustration, jealousy, and negative emotions that lead to real physical disorders. So closely are the body and mind intertwined that dishonoring one's parents — the very ones who brought you into the world — does indeed lead to disease and a shortened lifespan. So important is the matter of treating one's parents with love and respect that the Levitical law rewarded cursing or disrespecting one's father or mother with stoning (Exodus 21:17; Leviticus 20:9; Deuteronomy 20:16)! Families are meant to live in peace and harmony, children supporting their parents as they grow older and less firm. Jesus made this principle clear when He castigated the scribes and Pharisees.

"All too well you reject the commandment of God, that you may keep your tradition. For Moses said, 'Honor your father and your mother,' and 'He who curses father or mother, let him be put to death.' But you say, 'If a man says to his father or mother, "Whatever profit you might have received from me is Corban" (that is a gift to God), then you no longer let him do anything for his father or his mother, making the word of God of no effect through your tradition....'" (Mark 7:9-13).

Commandment 6. "You shall not murder." The very act of murder implies a state of mind that is corrupted with hate and vengeance towards one's fellow man, which S.I. McMillan assures us will lead to disease and early death. He stated in the opening paragraph of the preface to *None of These Diseases*,

"Peace does not come in capsules! This is regrettable because medical science recognizes that emotions such as fear, sorrow, envy, resentment, and hatred are responsible for the majority of our sicknesses. Estimates vary from 60 percent to nearly 100 percent."[31]

Not only is the life of the victim cut short, but the lives of everyone affected by the death are negatively impacted, leading to illness. Cain suffered the automatic agonies that accompany murder.

"So now you are cursed from the earth, which has opened its mouth to receive your brother's blood from your hand. When you till the ground, it shall no longer yield its strength to you. A fugitive and a vagabond you shall be on earth" (Genesis 4:11-12).

Moreover, the very thought of *hate* [Greek *miseo*, "regard with ill-will, detest, abhor"][32] towards one's brother makes you a murderer (I John 3:15). Once again, the very close association of ungodly thoughts with sickness and death leaps from the pages of God's word.

Commandment 7. "You shall not commit adultery" (Exodus 20:14). Having sexual relations with someone else's mate, committing fornication (sex before marriage), or practicing other forbidden sexual practices opens one up to a host of STDs that have already been discussed. Moreover, horrible diseases can be passed on from certain animals to men through bestiality, such as Ebola in Africa.[33] The animosity created among men and women due to adulterous affairs and pre-marital liaisons leads to bitterness, stress, and heartache, and thus physical and mental diseases.[34] Jesus made it clear that even to look lustfully upon one of the opposite sex [Greek *epithumeo*, "to have an earnest desire for"][35] is akin to committing adultery (Matthew 5:28). Such hurt within one's heart cannot lead to the harmony and love in life that promote health and longevity.

Commandment 8. "You shall not steal" (Exodus 20:15). The mindset required to steal someone else's property is in itself a recipe for disease. The conflict, anger, greed, and jealousy that move a person to steal lead to distress of body and mind, which S.I. Mc Millan tied so intimately to illness.[36] Let us not forget also the principle of stealing as related to foods themselves. By refining flour and other foods, much of the nutritional value — vitamins, minerals, and fiber — is removed, which leads to deficiencies of essential nutrients. Coupled

Foodless foods — those that are refined, adulterated, and stale — are the enemies of vibrant health, and need to be avoided. Sturdy, energetic bodies result from foods that are nutrient dense, fresh, and unprocessed.[38]

with the addition of preservatives, coloring agents, emulsifiers, artificial flavors, and other chemicals the native nutrition of foods is compromised — stolen from! Then figure in crop varieties such as hybrids and GMOs that further dilute nutrients with extra starches, and add toxins, plus crop fertilization practices that produce high yields of nutrient-deficient crops, which sit on store shelves for weeks or months, and a complete recipe of "foods having been stolen from" is set before the typical family.[37]

Commandment 9. "You shall not bear false witness against your neighbor" (Exodus 20:16). Lying to or about one's neighbor produces great stress and anger among fellow human beings. The issue does not only concern testimonies in a courtroom, but day-to-day associations with others in the home, at work, at play, or wherever people interact. A long, disease-free life cannot be expected for someone who languishes in heartache and guilt because he or she lied about someone or something. The effects of such false witnessing are automatic, and illness is the fruit.[39]

Commandment 10. "You shall not covet ..." (Exodus 20:17). *Coveting* [Hebrew *chamad*, "to lust, delight in, or are fond of either properly or improperly"][40] here refers to strongly wanting something that belongs to someone else: his house, mate, servant, livestock, or anything else he might possess that you believe would profit you, but which you cannot possess because you do not need it, cannot afford it, or it belongs to someone else. This commandment is in truth the precursor to most of the other commandments, for it is a morbid attitude that precedes worshipping false gods, stealing, murdering, and committing adultery. You want something you should not have. It is the state of mind that Ahab had when his wife Jezebel convinced him to expropriate Naboth's vineyard after she had Naboth killed (I Kings 21:1-16), that David had when taking notice of Bathsheba bathing and deciding to have her (II Samuel 11:1-4), and that Cain had when he desired the attention for his offering that Yahweh gave Abel, before Cain slew him (Genesis 4:3-5). Coveting leads to untold trouble and death, as these examples show.

The Statutes

In addition to the Ten Commandments, Yahweh put many statutes in place within the nation of Israel to insure long and abundant life. A few of these statutes are given below. **Clean and unclean meats.** Israel was commanded to eat only animals, birds, and fish that were considered "clean." These included mammals with cloven hooves that chewed the cud, fish that had fins and scales, seed-eating birds, and locusts. All other creatures were considered unclean, not fit for food, the reason being that their flesh was harmful to health and longevity. Thus, pigs, horses, rats, snakes, catfish, eagles, bats, and ants were all disallowed as food (Leviticus 11:1-30; Deuteronomy 14:3-20).

The facts about pork and shellfish being undesirable foods have already been discussed. The desire of our great God is to guide us through life in health and vigor into old age. We know we will someday die, since we have all sinned in the shadow of Adam, but we desire a long and relatively disease-free life, one blessed by the Creator because we follow His eternal laws. Remember the Fifth Commandment with a promise ... to have a long life on the earth.

Here are some of the statutes set forth for us to follow to promote long and healthful living. **The statute requiring the building of a parapet** (short fence) on the flat roof of one's house helps prevent accidental falls (Deuteronomy 22:8). **Keeping a dangerous ox under control** helps prevent accidental goring of an unsuspecting passerby (Exodus 21:28-31).

Avoiding unlawful sexual liaisons prevents the spread of STDs, and avoids the awful psychological consequences of lewd behavior (Leviticus 18 and 20; Deuteronomy 27:20-23). **Blood and fat.** No blood was to be consumed, but was to be poured out on the ground, and fat was to be avoided (Genesis 9:4; Leviticus 3:17; 7:26-27; 17:10-14; 19:26; Deuteronomy 12:16, 23; 15:23; Acts 21:25). The consumption of both blood and fat have very negative effects on the body.[41] **Laws of quarantine.** To avoid the spread of the disease of leprosy, strict statutes were in place to segregate those infected with the dreaded disease from the rest of the population (Leviticus 13 and 14). This principle of quarantine is useful for certain other communicable diseases as well. It is a major secret for containing contagious diseases that might otherwise devastate a population.[42]

None of These Diseases

We have explored the meaning of Exodus 15:26, which states that the Eternal God would not place the diseases of the Egyptians upon the Israelites if they would listen to His commandments and keep His statutes. The Decalogue, as well as many statutes based upon that royal law, do indeed protect people from illness and early death … if they will but keep them. We cannot avoid aging and ultimate death in the flesh due to sin having entered with Adam, but we can do so very much to live healthfully by following the basic laws of heath:

1. Eat clean meats and pure, nutrient dense foods, and drink pure water.
2. Exercise regularly and properly.
3. Get plenty of sunshine and fresh air.
4. Rest adequately.
5. Avoid accidents.
6. Practice good hygiene.
7. Think the positive thoughts of our Creator.

We have explored how keeping the laws of God leads to healthful living and the prevention of disease. But there is another very important facet of this promise so that we might avoid the afflictions of the Egyptians. Note the last sentence of Exodus 15:26: "For I am the Lord who *heals* [*rapha*, 'to heal, to be cured']."[44] We cannot avoid all sickness. That is impossible in this world. Yet, when we do become ill God has promised He will heal us! That promise was not afforded the Egyptians. Oh, the Egyptians had immune systems to fight off diseases just like the Israelites did, but they did not have the instructions from the commandments and statutes that aided their immune systems to throw off disease. Much more, they did not have the marvelous healing power of the Creator, the Yahweh Rapheka [God is our Healer], to cure them when sickness came.

See what James said.

"Is anyone among you sick? Let him call for

In spite of a person's best efforts to remain healthy, he still may become ill. Yet, there is the promise of our Creator to heal through the prayers of the faithful, the laying on of hands, and the faith of the afflicted.[43]

It is our living God who heals and sustains us, and pleads with us to obey His commandments and statutes so we will not become sick in the first place.

the elders of the church, and let them pray over him, anointing him with oil in the name of the Lord. And the prayer of faith will save the sick, and the Lord will raise him up. And if he has committed sins, he will be forgiven. Confess your trespasses to one another, and pray for one another, that you may be healed. The effective, fervent prayer of a righteous man avails much," (James 5:14-16).

As stated at the beginning of this chapter, Jesus Christ came "... that men may have life, and may have it in all its fullness" (John 10:10; TNEB). He wants us to avoid disease and remain in excellent health, but to do so requires a preventative approach against disease (note III John 2).

It is our great living God who heals and sustains us, and pleads with us to obey His commandments and statutes so we will not become sick in the first place. What greater love could our Creator have shown us than to reveal the ways to be in health and avoid disease … to have the joy, peace, energy, and vitality that Adam and Eve had in the Garden of Eden. What great love our Creator shows to us!

Fellowship of brethren united in the faith is like the precious anointing oil poured on the head of the high priest. The elect who possess God's spirit have this same gift when anointed with brethren dwelling together in unity.[2]

THE TENTH BRANCH

LOVE IS THE FELLOWSHIP OF THE SAINTS

A man decided one summer to join a pipeline company for a change of pace from his regular work. The first day on the job he was given a shovel and shown a particular plot of ground, and told to dig a trench six feet deep and three feet wide. By noon, he had dug down over his head and felt very much alone at his work. By the middle of the afternoon he was pretty discouraged as he thought of the miles of line still to be dug. Finally, however, about five o'clock, he broke through into the trench the man in front of him was digging. As he cleared away the loose dirt, this man broke through into the next hole, and as they stood and watched, man after man broke through to the adjoining trenches along the pipeline route until several hundred feet of completed ditch were visible. The work of all the ditch diggers working together towards a common goal gave the man a great sense of accomplishment. The "fellowship of the diggers" working in concert gave everyone much encouragement.[1]

Then there is the instruction of Paul in I Corinthians 14:23-26. He knew just how powerful fellowship could be when conducted properly, even converting unbelievers during a single visit! We cannot limit the power of God's intervention in the lives of those with whom we associate.

"So if the whole church comes together and everyone speaks in tongues, and some who are uninstructed or some unbelievers come in, will they not say that you are out of your minds! But if an unbeliever or uninstructed person comes in while everyone is prophesying, he will be convicted and called to account by all, and the secrets of his heart will be made known. So he will fall facedown and worship God, proclaiming, 'God is truly among you!' What then shall we say, brothers? When you come together, everyone has a psalm or a teaching, a revelation, a tongue, or an interpretation. All of these must be done to build up the *church* [*ecclesia*]."

Our heavenly Father granted a wonderful gift to us when He called us out of this world of sin, which brought us into fellowship with others of like mind. It is the *koinonia* ("partnership, communion")[2] that King David spoke about so glowingly in Psalm 133.

"Behold, how good and how pleasant it is for brethren to dwell together in unity! It is like the precious oil upon the head, running down on the beard, the beard of Aaron, running down on the edge of his garments. It is like the dew of Hermon, descending upon the mountains of Zion; for there the Lord commanded the blessing — life forevermore."

The love of brethren is a gift beyond comprehension! It is a foretaste of the communion we will have with one another for eternity, and let's face it: love cannot be expressed unless it is towards others. It is the outpouring of oneself to uplift others. We oftentimes take that reality for granted, but we ought not.

So, why is fellowship so important? The answer is in two broad brushstrokes: (1) encouragement for ourselves and others, and (2) expressing our spiritual gifts to one another. Let's examine these concepts and see just how important fellowship is in showing love to one another.

Living within a world filled with so much heartache and corruption — wars, disease, hurricanes, earthquakes, volcanoes, crime, abortion, infidelity, addictions, and the list goes on— wears down even the best intentions of those striving to serve the living God. We are surrounded by a plethora of troubles in all shapes and sizes, and they wear on us.

To combat these evil forces around us, we need the regular uplift of our brethren who are committed to putting off this evil, to help us face this unfriendly world and "... contend earnestly for the faith which was once for all delivered to the saints" (Jude 3). This *encouragement* [*parakaleo*, "to call to one's side, hence to call to one's aid, thus comfort, exhort, call for, to beseech"][4] is emphasized throughout the writings of Paul (Acts 14:22; 15:32; 16:40; 18:27; 20:1; Romans 11:2; I Corinthians 14:31; Ephesians 6:22; Colossians 2:2; 4:8; I Thessalonians 2:12; 4:18; 5:11, 14; I Timothy 5:1; Hebrews 10:25).

Encouragement among the brethren usually meets its greatest fulfillment during Sabbath and Holy Day events. These events are highlighted in Exodus 20:10-11, Leviticus 23:2-3, Isaiah 58:13-14, and elsewhere, and show us that the day has ten directives.

1. A holy convocation. *Holy* comes from *qodesh*, "a sacred place or thing."[5]
2. A Sabbath of rest; no work is to be done.

3. A Feast day, of both physical and spiritual food.
4. Do not do your own pleasure.
5. Make the day a delight. *Delight* is the Hebrew *oneg*, "pleasant, soft or pliable."[6]
6. Honor God in the day.
7. Do not speak your own words.
8. Reflect back to the Garden of Eden and the original creation.
9. A blessed day. *Blessed* comes from the Hebrew *barak*, "to kneel, to bless God as an act of adoration and to bless man."[7]
10. A hallowed day. *Hallowed* is the Hebrew *qadash*, "to be, make, observe, pronounce."[8]

These qualities of the day point towards life in the millennial reign of Jesus Christ, showing that the nature of the Sabbath is to live in Eden itself. It is the seventh day of the week, analogous to the seventh 1,000 years of mankind's tenure on earth… each day being as 1,000 prophetic years (II Peter 3:8; Psalm 90:4). We are to live during this day as if we are already there in that Kingdom realm.

> *The brethren are admonished to prophesy to one another — speak under divine inspiration — and thereby encourage each other with the gifts they have been given. Sharing those gifts is of profound importance.*[9]

The encouragement of the day is expedited, of course, through words, and how clear is the Apostle Paul in expressing the character of the day. Look at the progression of Paul's thoughts as he wrote in his first letter to the Corinthians, a progression that is obviously intended as he built up to the matter of Sabbath fellowship.

What is most fascinating here is that the chapter on fellowship — I Corinthians 14 — starts right off in verse 1 by saying, "Follow after love [in chapter 13], and desire spiritual gifts [in chapter 12], but rather that you prophesy."

The importance of respecting the wisdom and guidance of older people among the elect is underscored throughout the word of God. These older people are the "elders" as described by Paul and other disciples, and they do not represent an office in an organization.[13]

Paul is saying that *prophesying* [*propheteuo*], which in this context is "speaking under divine inspiration,"[10] is to be desired even above expressing love and spiritual gifts! What a profound statement, knowing the critical importance of both love and gifts! What is he saying?

He is saying that speaking messages to one another, as inspired by the holy spirit, is to be greatly desired. Why? Because these words are of vital importance for the encouragement of others in the group, providing messages in love to upbuild others using one's spiritual gifts. Note that this plea to the brethren to

prophesy is directed to all of the brethren, not just to a "minister" or "pastor."

The instructions for fellowship are as follows:

1. All things are to be done in order (I Corinthians 14:40).
2. Two or three people are to speak their inspired words, and the others are to *judge* [*diakrino*, "discriminate, oppose"][11] or "cross-examine" to ascertain the truth of a particular teaching (I Corinthians 14:29).
3. Spiritual gifts of everyone are to be freely expressed (I Corinthians 14:26).[12]
   Psalms (*psalmos*, "a set piece of music")

Doctrine (*didache*, "instruction or teaching")
Tongue [*glossa*, "a language, either known or unknown")
Revelation (*apokalupsis*, "disclosure")
Interpretation (*hermeneia*, "translation")

In all of these expressions the spirit of God is to flow freely, inspiring everyone to contribute during the gathering to encourage and uplift. Love must pervade the meeting, and spiritual gifts must be allowed their unfettered sharing ... and even as I Corinthians 14 began by encouraging everyone to prophesy, so the chapter closes by saying the same:

"Therefore, brethren, desire earnestly to prophesy, and do not forbid to speak with tongues" (I Corinthians 14:39).

Earnestly desire to prophesy! Earnestly desire to share knowledge of the truth with your brethren that you may encourage them. This action rolls up love and spiritual gifts together into one powerful package, which is surely a major reason why Paul encouraged prophesying so strongly.

It is important within fellowship to never allow a spirit of authoritarianism to enter. Jesus Christ washed the disciples' feet, even though He acknowledged He was Lord and Teacher (John 13:12-16), and Paul again acknowledged that Jesus considered others greater than Himself (Philippians 2:1-5). We likewise must never rule over others, for the essence of love is liberty and freedom (James 1:25-27).

Elders are not rulers and overlords appointed to an office by "ordination," but are older brethren [*presbyteros*, "a senior or older person"].[4] They are to be humble servants of others, able to uplift because of wisdom that accompanies age (Acts 20:28; I Peter 5:1-3). Do not be confused by scriptures like I Timothy 4:14 and Acts 14:23; older people in the congregations were sometimes appointed to fulfill certain functions based upon their inherent or spirit-appointed gifts. They could never be "made elders," for that would mean that laying hands on a person could add years to your age. Incidentally Timothy, though having hands laid on him by the older men of the fellowship to impart the gift of prophecy (inspired speaking; I Timothy 4:14), was not an elder. He was a young man, but a highly motivated servant of God (I Timothy 4:12).

Fellowship is indeed a wonderful gift bestowed upon the brethren for the sake of up-building the entire body of Christ. It is designed to encourage the brethren in a spirit of joy, to enable one's spiritual gifts to be shared with one another, to serve and bring about spiritual growth so that everyone might become more like the Creator and Jesus Christ, and reach ever upward towards the future kingship that is promised to those called out of this sin-stained world.

CONCLUSION

THE CONSEQUENCES OF FAILING TO PRACTICE LOVE

It is a fearsome thought to imagine a world without love, or a world where love wanes. Jesus Christ prophesied that in the end time, "… because lawlessness will abound, the *love* [*agape*] of many will grow cold" (Matthew 24:12). Because of that the Great Tribulation will rise and much of the world's population will die. We see here a direct connection between lawlessness and a lack of love, as we discussed earlier.

Breaking God's laws leads to hatred and trouble on every side. Love is the glue, as it were, that binds families, communities, and nations together. As Pawel Skibinski, one of Poland's top historians, stated,

"A strong family is necessary for any community. If you want to have a strong society, you have to have a

Marital love is the direct reflection of the Creator's love for each of His chosen elect, His bride. We love Him, we cherish Him, and will do everything we can to please Him, just as the wife desires to please her husband.[2]

strong family first. It is no coincidence that those who want to destroy society attack the family first.

"If one agrees that one is both an individual and a member of society, then one realizes that one has obligations to the community. If that disappears, then society will fall apart. Any sense of love will disappear, because society is based on love."[1]

We can go a giant step further and surmise that virtually *nothing* could exist without love: God is love (I John 4:8), and through love He binds all things together and sustains them. All things were brought into existence because of His mind ... which has love at its core. His words — frequencies of energy, we may put it — spoke things into being during the creation week (John 1:1-3; Psalm 33:6; Ephesians 3:9; Colossians 1:16; Hebrews 1:2; Revelation 4:11): light, water, the heavens and its gases, the sun, moon, and stars, plants, animals, birds, fish, and man (Genesis 1:3, 7, 8, 11, 14, 20, 24, 26). He "... upholds all things by the word of His power" (Hebrews 1:3).

The words of Rolf Witzche put the matter into excellent perspective.

"An atom is empty space in which a miracle unfolds. Nuclear physics tells us that the entire universe contains not a single speck of matter, not even in the smallest part of the smallest atom, but is the construct of energy and its forces that have been arranged in a complex array of harmonizing principles without which the universe simply would not exist.

"At the center of the empty space that makes up an atom is a grouping of infinitesimally small 'particles' located that is surrounded by an orbiting 'swarm' of even smaller particles. Their movement is so fast that they

Matter is composed of atoms, and atoms in turn are comprised of electrons, protons, and neutrons. Ultimately, these particles are probably subdivided infinitely, all of them originating from the omnipotent energy that pervades the entire universe and takes its various forms through the motions they encapsulate.[4]

appear to be everywhere at once, creating the appearance of a solid sphere. However, the so-called particles don't exist either as solid entities, but are themselves constructs of various types of what the physicists call quarks, which are defined as but fast moving points of energy.

"Thus, there exists no such thing as basic matter or basic particles. Everything that we see, hear, or touch, even the world we live in, is but the construct of patterns of energy organized by harmonizing principles that altogether reveal an underlying arrangement of an incredible Intelligence. If one of the harmonizing principles was missing, or antagonistic to the whole, the universe would have no foundation to exist, and so it wouldn't exist. But it does exist. It exists as the product of an incredible Intelligence and its harmonizing 'Spirit' that might be termed 'Love.' Outside of these there is nothing. The only basic building blocks in the universe are Intelligence and its harmonizing 'Spirit.' And ultimately, there remains but one, which is Intelligence and its 'Spirit' that is Love."[3]

A volume published by Dewey B. Larson in 1959 entitled *Nothing But Motion* defined the physical universe in terms of motion as well, stating that space and time are simply the two reciprocal aspects of motion ... that matter as science has defined it does not exist.

"The thesis of this present work is that the universe in which we live is not a universe of matter, but a *universe of motion*, one in which the basic reality is motion, and all physical entities and phenomena, including matter, are merely manifestations of motion. The atom, on this basis, is simply a combination of motions. Radiation is motion, gravitation is motion, an electric charge is motion, and so on."[5]

Larson goes on to describe that this motion (velocity) is defined by space and time, the simple $v = s/t$ equation, where v=velocity, s=space (dimension), and t=time,[6] so we may suppose that Elohim, by speaking frequencies (motion), created what we term matter in its various forms of elements, compounds, minerals, organic constructs, and living beings, as well as the entire electromagnetic spectrum. These things would all be brought into being by motion — assumedly vortical — within the sea of energy throughout the universe. As Larson states, "Without motion there would be no universe."[7]

Dewey Larson, without totally understanding what he was saying, hit upon the very essence of God's design of things: taking formless energy and shaping it into the multitudes of components that comprise this physical world. The mind, words, and frequencies of the Eternal combined to produce the reality we see and sense around us. Since God is love, the forms we sense are a direct reflection of that spirit quality ... too wonderful for us to comprehend as limited human beings, but reality nonetheless.

Let us return from the reality of the physical universe and all that we see around us — constructed and maintained by God's love — to us human beings, with our families, communities, and nations. It is the interrelationships among us all that define our existence: joyful, miserable, or somewhere between. We have seen how governmental structure has everything to do with the expression of love and joy amongst citizens of a family, a community, and a nation. Communistic, totalitarian states suppress the expression of that natural love by squelching the free expression of individual liberties and try to force people to obey and worship, as it were, the State, in particular the dictator in charge, such as the premier of North Korea, the president of Venezuela, or the leader of China … who even sometimes claim they are gods themselves as did the Pharaohs in Egypt, and Nimrod way back in Babylon (Genesis 10:8-9). These tyrants fail to comprehend that, by virtue of their birth, all human beings are intended to be sovereign before God with innate, God-plane privileges.

This central truth of existence was understood by the founding fathers of the United States when they penned the Declaration of Independence, and were willing to face the inevitable fury of the British army to try and extinguish the flames of liberty within the fledgling nation.

"We hold these Truths to be self-evident, that all Men are created equal, that they are endowed by their Creator with certain unalienable Rights, that among these are Life, Liberty, and the Pursuit of Happiness — That to secure these Rights, Governments are instituted among Men, deriving their just Powers from the Consent of the Governed, that whenever any form of Government becomes destructive of these Ends, it is the Right of the People to alter or to abolish it, and to institute new Government, laying its Foundation on such Principles, and organizing its Powers in such form, as to them shall seem most likely to affect their Safety and Happiness. Prudence, indeed, will dictate that Governments long established should not be changed for light and transient Causes; and accordingly, all Experience hath shewn, that Mankind are more disposed to suffer, while Evils are sufferable, than to right themselves by abolishing the forms to which they are accustomed. But when a long Train of Abuses and Usurpations, pursuing invariably the same Object, evinces a Design to reduce them under absolute Despotism, it is their Right, it is their Duty, to throw off such Government, and to provide new Guards for their future Security. Such has been the patient Sufferance of these Colonies; and such is now the Necessity which constrains them to alter their former Systems of Government. The History of the present King of Great Britain is a History of repeated

Injuries and Usurpation, all having in direct Object the Establishment of an absolute Tyranny over these States. To prove this, let Facts be submitted to a candid World."[8]

Franklin, Jefferson, Adams and others who framed this amazing document admitted that …

1. God provided life, liberty, and the pursuit of happiness (in earlier versions that term was "property") inherent to every newborn person as God-given rights.

2. It is natural for people to suffer oppression by a subjugating government when those rights are suppressed.

3. People who are so oppressed that they can no longer exercise a reasonable degree of freedom in their lives must throw off such an oppressive government, and forge a new life based on the liberties God intends for them.

We know that despotic leaders of any sort live under the tutelage of the Adversary, whose intent is to remove love from leadership and force citizens to bow down to another human being. The fervor of the American colonists conspired to cast off the yoke of British oppression and live in liberty, under a system of government that guaranteed liberty to individuals, which eventually was codified in the Constitution that was ratified a few years after the Declaration of Independence in 1788.[10]

These remarkable documents initiated a Constitutional Republic that strove to guarantee love as the object of government: to keep the oppressive hierarchy at bay by dividing the governing system into Legislative, Executive, and Judicial branches to lessen the chances for a despot to gain power, as occurred in England. This yearning for liberty is the same for all of humanity, whose desire is to claim their God-given birthright so eruditely stated by Jesus Christ.

The Constitutional Convention during the formation of the United States brought together delegates from the thirteen colonies, the personalities that God worked through to provide a Constitution based upon eternal living laws of love, giving us the freedoms we enjoy even to this day.[9]

"Come to Me, all you who labor and are heavy laden, and I will give you rest. Take My yoke upon you and learn from Me, for I am gentle and lowly in heart, and you will find rest for your souls. For My yoke is easy and My burden is light" (Matthew 11:28-30).

How similar this quote is to Paul's statement in I John 5:3: "For this is the love of God, that you keep His commandments; and His commandments are not burdensome."

Prophecy has predicted a coming government ruled by what is termed the Beast and the False Prophet, despots of the secular and religious facets of a one-world government who will strive to subject everyone on planet earth to bow down to its authority. The means by which this will happen will be a system of control by the Beast, and the Image of the Beast.

"He was granted power to give breath to the image of the beast, that the image of the beast should both speak and cause as many as would not worship the image of the beast to be killed. He causes all, both small and great, rich and poor, free and slave, to receive a mark on their right hand or on their foreheads, and that no one may buy or sell except one who has the mark or the name of the beast, or the number of his name. Here is wisdom. Let him who has understanding calculate the number of the beast, for it is the number of a man: his number is 666" (Revelation 13:15-18).

Satan the devil, who is fomenting technology at this very moment through several educational institutions and companies, to create an electronic computerized system that will place a mark of some sort on each person, to control sales or purchases, will attempt to make slaves of everyone … and those who will not comply he will try to kill.[11] This effort is very much like what was predicted in George Orwell's novel *1984*.[12] Let us take a closer look at this book as articulated in "A World Without Love: The Ramifications of An Affectionless Society in 1984."

"It is important to highlight the isolation manifestations from their members. Instead of love, the party promotes hate among people during the Two Minutes' Hate on a daily basis.
"In fact, the Ministry of Love was ironically the most dangerous and scariest ministry of all, as Winston says: 'The Ministry of Love was the very frightening one. There were no windows in it at all.' The quote shows how the ministry of love, contrary to what love represents, looks detrimental and dark portraying an isolated, cold sensation. Winston noticed the incongruences between the Party point of view about love, and what he felt love was from the vague memory from his past where he has a feeling that makes him believe love and other emotions were present in the past; he says those feelings '… belonged to the ancient time,

to a time when there was still privacy, love, and friendship.'

"The party suppressed love and relationships because they lose power, and people lose focus from Big Brother. An irony surrounds the party as it battles love, but all the inner party members seem to be in love with Brother's ideology. In fact, when they want to 'rehabilitate' a rebel, they seek for him to love Big Brother. This is what happens to Winston at the very end of the novel. The physical and psychological torture make him forget real love to develop a fake love towards Big Brother. 'He had won the victory over himself. He loved Big Brother.' Winston at the end suppressed the love he had for Julia, and incorporates the falsity of an introduced love. He loses all his freedom of loving and caring about Julia, and at the same time he loses his awareness and his sanity which develops in the addiction to gin and the return of his pain and sickness. "The lack of love in 1984 portrays a lack of compassion, solidarism, and care for the majority of the members of the party. The party tries to dehumanize people in all possible ways to keep them slaves of the party to maintain control. This control is exerted through psychological and physical torture. For example, in the ministry of love people were tortured to a point they would do anything to escape. 'Finish it off and let me die. Shoot me. Hang me …. Is there somebody else you want me to give away?

…. I don't care who it is or what you do to them. I've got a wife and three children. The biggest of them isn't six years old. You can take the whole lot of them and cut their throats in front of my eyes, and I'll stand by and watch it. But not Room 1011.' Here the party tortures an old man to the point that he is willing to do whatever they ask."[13]

Whether a society such as portrayed in 1984 could ever develop is questionable, but the history of civilization is rife with programs of torture to force people to convert — such as the Inquisition — or to move people toward a specified way of thinking, using the Hegelian Dialectic.[15] All of these systems of forcing people to worship men and renounce the Source of love are doomed to failure, of course. They are counter to the very essence of who we are.

The consequences of failing to practice love are heartache, suffering, sickness, and lack of fulfillment. They are the pathway of wickedness. Oh, the wicked may prosper for a time, as Job and others made clear (Job 12:6; 21:13; Psalm 73:3; Jeremiah 12:1), but in the end they must answer for everything they do, and their end is not what anyone desires … especially for the wicked themselves. The ultimate consequence of failing to practice love is the collapse of civilization, for all societies prosper or disintegrate in proportion to the degree that they practice pure, unfettered love. We see this in the "blessings and cursings" chapters: Leviticus 26 and Deuteronomy 28.

Without the free expression of love within a society the roots of totalitarianism soon take hold, and drive out the bedrock of truth, kindness, humility, and goodness, leaving a people subjugated to the whims of other men who exert power over others. Those who will not bow down are either forcibly reeducated or exterminated.[14]

Where are we along the timeline of prophecy? Are we within the period of the seals of Revelation 6 — the Four Horsemen of the Apocalypse — which was also reviewed by Jesus Christ in Matthew 24? Judge for yourself.

"Now as He sat on the Mount of Olives, the disciples came to Him privately, saying, 'Tell us, when will these things be? And what will be the sign of Your coming, and of the end of the age?' And Jesus answered and said to them: 'Take heed that no one deceives you. For many will come in My name, saying, "I am the Christ," and will deceive many. And you will hear of wars and rumors of wars. See that you are not troubled; for all these things must come to pass, but the end is not yet. For nation will rise against nation, and kingdom against kingdom. And there will be famines, pestilences, and earthquakes in various places. All these are the beginning of sorrows. Then they will deliver you up to tribulation and kill you, and you will be hated by all nations for My name's sake. And then many will be offended, will betray one another, and will hate one another. Then many false prophets will rise up and deceive many. ***And because lawlessness will abound, the love of many will grow cold.*** But he who endures to the end shall be saved. And this gospel of the kingdom will be preached in all the world as a witness to all the nations, and then the end will come" (Matthew 24:3-13; emphasis mine).

We are told by the Messiah that most people will have lost their natural love for one another at the end of the age. Notice this truth through the words of Isaiah 24, when during the Tribulation great atrocities against people of all nations will be committed, and few men will survive to live into the coming age.

"Behold, the Lord makes the earth empty and makes it waste, distorts its surface, and scatters abroad its inhabitants.

And it shall be: as with the people, so with the priest; as with the servant, so with his master; as with the maid, so with her mistress; as with the buyer, so with the seller; as with the lender, so with the borrower; as with the creditor, so with the debtor.

"The land shall be entirely emptied and utterly plundered, for the Lord has spoken this word. The earth mourns and fades away, the world languishes and fades away; the haughty people of the earth languish.

"The earth is also defiled under its inhabitants, because they have transgressed the laws, changed the ordinance, broken the everlasting covenant. Therefore the curse has devoured the earth, and those who dwell in it are desolate. Therefore the inhabitants of the earth are burned, and few men are left.

"The new wine fails, the vine languishes, all the merry-hearted sigh. The mirth of the tambourine ceases, the noise of the jubilant ends, the joy of the harp ceases. They shall not drink wine with a song; strong drink is bitter to those who drink it.

'The city of confusion is broken down; every house is shut up, so that none may go in. There is a cry for wine in the streets, all joy is darkened, the mirth of the land is gone.

"In the city desolation is left, and the gate is stricken with destruction. When it shall be thus in the midst of the land among the people, it shall be like the shaking of an olive tree, like the gleaning of grapes when the vintage is done. They shall lift up their voice, they shall sing; for the majesty of the Lord they shall cry aloud from the sea. Therefore glorify the Lord in the dawning light, the name of the Lord God of Israel in the coastlands of the sea.

"From the ends of the earth we have heard songs: 'Glory to the righteous!' But I said, 'I am ruined, ruined! Woe to me! The treacherous dealers have dealt treacherously, indeed, the treacherous dealers have dealt very treacherously.'

The end result of a loveless society is destruction, not only of people and families but of the entire earth. This is the end that the adversary desires, but it is the end that all of us need to forever combat.[16]

"Fear and the pit and the snare are upon you, O inhabitant of the earth. And it shall be that he who flees from the noise of the fear shall fall into the pit, and he who comes up from the midst of the pit shall be caught in the snare;

"For the windows from on high are open, and the foundations of the earth are shaken. The earth is violently broken, the earth is split open, the earth is shaken exceedingly. The earth shall reel to and fro like a drunkard, and shall totter like a hut; its transgression shall be heavy upon it, and it will fall, and not rise again.

"It shall come to pass in that day that the Lord will punish on high the host of exalted ones, and on the earth the kings of the earth. They will be gathered together, as prisoners are gathered in the pit, and will be shut up in the prison; after many days they will be punished.

"Then the moon will be disgraced and the sun ashamed; for the Lord of hosts will reign on Mount Zion and in Jerusalem, and before His elders gloriously."

In spite of this carnage there is incredible hope on the other side of the soon-coming worldwide destruction of our Babylonian system, that system of religion, government, education, and commerce that has overspread the entire earth, one that is based on hierarchical rulership over nations and in churches, forced government schooling,

and shipping and trading based on digitized money, enriching the shipping magnates who are called the great men of the earth (Revelation 18:16-23). These rich men follow the lead of the Adversary himself, whose first sin was selfish merchandising, hoarding goods and power to himself (Ezekiel 28:16-18). Within the context of this lavish lifestyle of the rich and oppression of the poor, whose labors this Babylonian system exploit, there is hardly any room for love.

"Come now, you rich, weep and howl for your miseries that are coming upon you! Your riches are corrupted, and your garments are moth-eaten. Your gold and silver are corroded, and their corrosion will be a witness against you and will eat your flesh like fire. You have heaped up treasure in the last days. Indeed the wages of the laborers who mowed your fields, which you kept back by fraud, cry out; and the cries of the reapers have reached the ears of the Lord of Sabaoth. You have lived on the earth in pleasure and luxury; you have fattened your hearts as in a day of slaughter. You have condemned, you have murdered the just; he does not resist you" (James 5:1-6).

The inborn craving within every human creation for the love that God desires, and as the framers of the United States Constitution so ably declared —life, liberty, and the pursuit of happiness — can hardly be expressed within a system where people are ruled by other people. Every person is designed to be directly connected with his or her Creator. Our heavenly Father created each of us because of love — He must expand that love endlessly — and we need to grasp how wonderful a truth that is.

I have tried to show you through these ten chapters the various aspects of the Eternal's love for us. These cannot be separated from one another, but by examining each one and then combining them it is possible to gain a deeper understanding of the awesome, infinite care our true Daddy has for us. I have shown you through ten branches of a vine how expansive this love is.

1. The Ten Commandments
2. Fruits of the spirit
3. Laying down your life
4. God multiplying Himself
5. Living God's government
6. The least is the greatest
7. Revealed in marriage
8. Revealed in the creation
9. Granting health and fulfillment
10. Fellowship of the saints

Let us latch on to that love, understand it, live it, and endure with it to the end of this sin-filled age. Let us not succumb to the temptation to lose our grasp on salvation through the wars, famines, weather upsets, religious persecutions, threats of torture and death, and the lawlessness that characterizes this current age, as prophesied in II Timothy 3:1-3. Because of this lawlessness the love of many will wax cold. Do not become a part of those "many," but reject this world's insanity and endure to the end ... for "He that endures to the end shall be saved" (Matthew 24:13).

Moreover, Jesus Christ answered a certain lawyer who wanted to test Him about what one should do to inherit eternal life. Here is how our Messiah handled the question ... by asking another question: "What is written in the law? What is your reading of it?" Here is how the lawyer answered:

"You shall love the Lord your God with all your heart, with all your soul, and with all your strength, and with all your mind, and your neighbor as yourself" (Luke 10:27).

Jesus answered him, "You have answered rightly; do this and you will live" (verse 28). Love, love, and love some more, but on the Creator's terms as revealed in His words.

The road that we tread is a narrow and difficult pathway that few find (Matthew 7:13). Let us meet on that road and help one another stay on it. The Millennial Kingdom at the end will be worth every last bit of effort you make to keep your footing!

The least the greatest

Living His government

Foundation of marriage

God multiplying Himself

Revealed in the creation

Giving your life

Health and fulfillment

Fruits of the spirit

Fellowship

Ten Commandments

The Ten Branches of Love

EPILOGUE

WHY AM I HERE ON THIS EARTH?

I t has taken me a very long time to come to this point … to be able to finally put into words this matter that has plagued me for as long as I can remember. Why am I here on this earth? What is my purpose?

These questions are basic to existence, and I thought I had them answered, answered quite fully so I could move forward in life and fill in the remaining blanks as the months and years passed — no big deal. Man is made in the express image of Elohim Himself so that he might, upon being called and chosen, having repented of his evil ways, then be baptized, have hands laid on him, and receive the holy spirit, thereupon be destined for rulership in the

Kingdom (government) of God in a renewed earth.

It is a brilliant plan, one beyond the comprehension of man, to make us brothers of Jesus Christ, on the same spiritual plane, and with an inheritance like His. What a future to behold!

Yet, as time passed it became apparent there was a central understanding missing in my comprehension of this great future laid out plainly in Scripture. What was missing? Yes, a future as a king and priest in the coming Kingdom of God is the reality; it will come. So, is this not great beyond compare?

Indeed it is, but what is greatness, and what is the meaning behind it all. God's elect will reign as Kings and Priests on a renewed earth. We were made for this profound purpose, and we will live out the fullness of this plan in its entirety. Once we are there the responsibilities as leaders in the next age will be profound, exciting beyond imagination — but what is the profundity of it all? Will this exalted position not become commonplace and mundane in time? Will not the inability to sin lose its glamor, and life even in the spirit become passe?

Something was missing from my understanding, for I knew that Paul said we will be joint-heirs with Christ of the Kingdom,

"... if indeed we suffer with Him, that we may also be glorified together. For I consider that the sufferings of this present time are not

Love, I have come to understand, is a concept that engulfs the entire being, both sides of the brain, one might say. It ought to consume all that we are.

worthy to be compared with the glory which shall be revealed in us" (Romans 8:17-18; NKJV).

Besides this Paul stated,

"Eye has not seen, nor ear heard, nor have entered into the heart of man the things **which God has prepared for those who love Him**" (I Corinthians 2:9; see also Isaiah 64:4; 65:17; NKJV; emphasis mine).

Ah, that all-important qualifier: the things prepared for those who *love* Him. Everything of my future inheritance hinges upon my *love* for my elder Brother, Jesus Christ.

This leads to the obvious question: What does it mean to love? If one does not have it, then one cannot expect to receive those things God has prepared ... that is, kingship and priesthoodship in the Kingdom of God. A PERSON MUST UNDERSTAND AND PRACTICE LOVE! That love, as revealed in the very next verse, verse 10 of I Corinthians 2, is tied closely to the spirit of God in the elect, for it says, "But God has revealed them [the things He has prepared for those who love Him] to us through His spirit. For the spirit searches all things, yes, the deep things of God."

There you have it! The missing ingredient, as it were, in this all-consuming quest for understanding what is missing in the future prophetic reality of which I will be a partaker, depends utterly on practicing love.

Love, I have come to understand, is a concept that engulfs the entire being, both sides of the brain, one might say. It ought to consume all that we are.

I have often wondered why God has placed this need to understand love in such sharp focus within me. Perhaps the answer resides in my own shortcomings of not having been reared in a warm and loving home, where my father and mother did not surround me with much kindness and encouragement ... at least they were not obvious to me. Thus deprived of a well-grounded understanding of this close attachment and security to one's own parents, I was forced to examine the essentials of this quality — why some seemed to have it and others did not. I was moved to dissect this profoundly important quality of character that is obviously so important, but which so few seem to themselves understand, especially in this society filled with broken homes and one-parent families.

The need of love and care from one's physical parents is inborn. If not fulfilled by one's real or adoptive father and mother, then others must fill the void. Special friends stepped in to help fill the vacuum at an early age. I recall special contact with my heavenly Father, who saved me through several situations that could easily have proven fatal. It is the love of one's true spiritual Father that is so essential to living life as it ought to be, and to unveil this matter of love in all of its intricacies.

So I have come to the point in life where I wish to share with you my understanding of what love truly is. Love is the basis of the life we must live in relation to our Creator, to our fellow man — especially within our own families — and to the plant and animal creations around us. It is the character quality that must surround us and permeate us always, to cast out fear, selfishness, pride, and jealousy which battle against it. It is the trait which one must possess in order to be a King and Priest in the next age, and which one must understand and practice today to live an abundant life in dedication to the Creator.

Paul W, Syltie
December 30, 2020

END NOTES

Preface
1. Picture from *www.jw.org.*
2. *https://biblehub.com/greek/3313.htm.*

Introduction
1. Picture from the author, constructed by Abigail Evans, *www.abigailsyltieart.com.*
2. James Strong, *The Strong's Expanded Exhaustive Concordance of the Bible,* contributions by John R. Kohlenberger, III. Thomas Nelson Publishers, Nashville, Tennessee. 2001.
3. See 1.
4. See 1.
5. Deuteronomy 6:15; 10:12; 11:1, 13, 22; 13:3; 19:9; 30:6, 16, 20; Joshua 22:5; 23:11; Matthew 22:37; Mark 12:30; Luke 10:27; many others.

The First Branch: Love Is Implicit in the Ten Commandments
1. Photo from *www.globalyoungvoices.com.*
2. Note the article by Wendy Patrick, Are you more likely to meet dark personalities at night? *Psychology Today,* November 7, 2020, *www.psychologytoday.com.*
3. This story is taken from my undergraduate days at the University of Minnesota, St. Paul Campus.
4. The Ten Commandments may be found in Exodus 20:1-17, and Deuteronomy 5:6-21.
5. Photo from *www.jw.org.*
6. Warren Baker (editor), *The Complete Word Study Old Testament,* AMG Publishers, Chattanooga, Tennessee, 1994, page 9 of the Hebrew and Chaldee Dictionary.
7. Spiros Zodhiates (editor), *The Complete Word Study New Testament,* AMG Publishers, Chattanooga, Tennessee, 1991, page 58 of the Greek Dictionary of the New Testament.
8. See 7, page 37.
9. Picture from *www. growingchristianresources.com.*
10. See 6, page 24.
11. Bible Ask personnel, Was the law of Moses placed inside or outside the Ark of the covenant?, *www.bibleask.org/was-the-law-of-moses-placed-inside-or-outside-the-ark-of-the-covenant/.*
12. Picture from *www.goodfon.com.*

The Second Branch: Love Is a Fruit if the Spirit
1. Picture from *www.lovesongtomylife.com.*
2. Picture from *www.standard.net.*
3. Luke 15:21.

4. Luke 15: 22-24.

5. The process of our Father's calling is miraculous beyond comprehension, and is possible only because of the Father's intervention to draw a person out of this evil world, and set him on a course toward eternal life through the blood of the Messiah (John 6:44). Of those whom the Eternal has called and chosen, He grants His spirit to those who repent of their past evil ways, and directs them in a new way towards eternal life. The act of immersion in water to symbolically wash away sins, and the laying on of hands to impart the holy spirit, is a most profound experience that initiates the elect into the fellowship of the saints .

6. James Strong, *The New Strong's Expanded Exhaustive Concordance of the Bible,* edited by John Kohlenberger, III, Thomas Nelson, Nashville, Tennessee, 2001, page 2 of the Greek Dictionary of the New Testament, page 2.

7. Stephen Kosslyn and G. Wayne Miller, Left brain, right brain: two sides, always working together, *Psychology Today,* May 7, 2014, *www.psychologytoday.com.*

8. Picture from *www.freepic.com.*

The Third Branch: Love Is Laying Down Your Life

1. Picture from Avro Lancaster, *Wikipedia,* December 11, 2020, *en.wikipedia.org.*

2. Marlexander, War stories: the touching story of Holmes, 2020, *ng.operanews.com.*

3. Picture from *www.friendsofjehovahswitnesses.com.*

4. Picture from What are some ways I can make elderly people feel needed? *www.wisegeek.com.*

5. Picture from *www.jwsurvey.org.*

6. Spiros Zodhiates (editor), *The Complete Word Study New Testament,* AMG Publishers, Chattanooga, Tennessee, 1991, page 38 of the Greek Dictionary of the New Testament.

7. Photo from *www.pyramidhealthcarepa.com.*

8. Spiros Zodhiates (editor), *The Complete Word Study New Testement,* AMG Publishers, Chattanooga, Tennessee, 1991, page 71 of the Greek Dictionary of the New Testament.

The Fourth Branch: Love Is God Multiplying Himself

1. Warren Baker (editor), *The Complete Word Study Old Testament,* AMG Publishers, Chattanooga, Tennessee, 1991, page 71 of the Hebrew and Chaldee Dictionary

2. Photo from *Alabama Today,* February 19, 2018, *www.altoday.com.*

3. See 1, page 99.

4. Spiros Zodhiates (editor), *The Complete Word Study New Testament,* AMG Publishers, Chattanooga, Tennessee, 1991, page 53 of the Greek Dictionary of the New Testament.

5. Photo from *www.jw.org.*

6. See 1, page 80.

7. Photo from *www.thesun.co.uk.*

8. **WE ARE DESTINED TO RECEIVE**

RULERSHIP OVER THE NATIONS AS SPIRITS.

Jesus Christ and the Elect
"And I bestow upon you a kingdom, just as My Father bestowed one upon Me." (Luke 22:29).

Jesus Christ
Jesus Christ has received power to rule over the nations, just as will the saints (Revelation 2:26-27).
"And the armies in heaven, clothed in fine linen, white and clean, followed Him on white horses. Now out of His mouth goes a sharp sword, that with it He should strike the nations. And He Himself will rule them with a rod of iron.... And He has on His robe and on His thigh a name written: KING OF KINGS AND LORD OF LORDS" (Revelation 19:14-16).
"You say rightly that I am a king. For this cause I was born, and for this cause I have come into the world, that I should bear witness to the truth" (John 18:37).

The Elect
"Arise, shine:
For your [the elect's] light has come!
And the glory of the Lord is risen upon you.
For behold, the darkness shall cover the earth,
And deep darkness the people;
But the Lord will arise over you,
And His glory will be seen upon you.
The Gentiles shall come to your light,

And kings to the brightness of your rising" (Isaiah 60:1-3).

"And he who overcomes, and keeps My works until the end, to him I will give power over the nations — He shall rule them with a rod of iron; they shall be dashed to pieces like the potter's vessels [Psalm 2:9] — as I also have received from My Father ..." (Revelation 2:26-27).
"... For you were slain, and have redeemed us to God by Your blood out of every tribe and tongue and people and nation, and have made us kings and priests to our God; and we [the elect] shall reign on the earth" (Revelation 5:9-10).

10. WE ARE TO INHERIT ALL THINGS.

Jesus Christ
"'The silver is Mine, and the gold is Mine,' says the Lord of hosts" (Haggai 2:8).
"All things were made through Him [Christ], and without Him nothing was made that was made" (John 1:3).
"Of old You laid the foundation of the earth, and the heavens are the work of Your hands" (Psalm 102:25).
"I have made the earth, and created man on it. It was I — My hands — stretched out the heavens, and all their host I have commanded" (Isaiah 45:12).
"... which from the beginning of the ages has been hidden in God who created all things through Jesus Christ" (Ephesians 3:9).

"He is the image of the invisible God, the firstborn over all creation. For by Him all things were created that are in heaven and that are on earth, visible and invisible, whether thrones or dominions or principalities or powers. All things were created through Him and for Him. And He is before all things, and in Him all things consist" (Colossians 1:15-17).

"... Jesus, knowing that the Father had given all things into His hands ... (John 13:3).

The Elect

"He who overcomes shall inherit all things, and I will be his God and he shall be My son" (Revelation 21:7).

"Blessed are the poor in spirit for theirs is the kingdom of heaven.... Blessed are the meek, for they shall inherit the earth" (Matthew 5:3, 5).

"When I consider Your heavens, the work of Your fingers, the moon and the stars, which You have ordained, what is man that you are mindful of him, and the son of man that you visit him? For You have made him a little [while] lower than the angels, and you have crowned him with glory and honor. You have made him to have dominion over the works of Your hands; you have put all things under his feet ..." (Psalm 8:3-6).

11. WE RECEIVE GOD'S SPIRIT BY BAPTISM AND THE LAYING ON OF HANDS.

Jesus Christ

"When He had been baptized, Jesus came up immediately from the water; and behold, the heavens were opened to Him, and He saw the Spirit of God descending like a dove and alighting upon Him" (Matthew 3:16; see also Mark 1:10 and Luke 3:21-22).

Jesus was baptized along with a number of other people; see Luke 3:21. Like for the elect, God's holy spirit was given at baptism, for it is pictured descending as a dove, a dramatic demonstration of the Father's spirit-impregnating power. Such signs seldom accompany the baptism of the saints, but God's spirit is granted nonetheless. Jesus Christ's sinless life resulted from His strength of mind, body, and human spirit, in touch with His Father, bequeathed through direct birth from the Father, without the inherited faults of sinful preceding generations of fathers and mothers.

The Elect

"Repent, and let every one of you be baptized in the name of Jesus Christ for the remission of sins; and you shall receive the gift of the Holy Spirit" (Acts 2:38).

"And Ananias went his way and entered the house; and laying his hands on him he said, 'Brother Saul, the Lord Jesus, who appeared to you on the road as you came, has sent me that you may receive your sight and be filled with the holy spirit.'

Immediately there fell from his eyes something like scales, and he received his sight at once; and he arose and was baptized" (Acts 9:17-18).

"When they heard this, they were baptized in the name of the Lord Jesus. And when Paul had laid hands on them, the holy spirit came upon them, and they spoke with tongues and prophesied" (Acts 19:5-6).

"Do not neglect the gift that is in you, which was given to you by prophecy with the laying on of the hands of the eldership" (I Timothy 4:14).

12. WE ARE SPIRITUAL BROTHERS, WITH THE SAME FATHER, FAMILY, AND POTENTIAL.

Jesus Christ

"Then one said to Him, 'Look, Your mother and Your brothers are standing outside, seeking to speak with You.' But He answered and said to the one who told Him, 'Who is My mother and who are My brothers?' And He stretched out His hand toward His disciples and said, 'Here are My mother and My brothers!'" (Matthew 12:47-49).

"For whom He foreknew, He also predestined to be conformed to the image of His Son, that He might be the firstborn among many brethren" (Romans 8:29).

"I came forth from the Father and have come into the world. Again, I leave the world and go to the Father" (John 16:28).

"... Jesus Christ, the faithful witness, the firstborn from the dead ..." (Revelation 1:5).

As an Elder Brother whose mission it was to live a sinless life, and pay the penalty for men's sins as the pioneer or forerunner of the saints' salvation, Jesus Christ is the mediator between the elect and the Father (I Timothy 2:5), a function the elect could never perform at this time.

The Elect

"... that they all may be one, as You, Father, are in Me, and I in You; that they also may be one in Us, that the world may believe that You sent Me" (John 17:21).

"And He is the head of the body, the church, who is the beginning, the firstborn from the dead, that in all things He may have the preeminence" (Colossians 1:18).

"For both He who sanctifies and those who are being sanctified are all of one, for which reason He is not ashamed to call them brethren .... And again: 'Here am I and the children whom God has given Me'" [Isaiah 8:18]" (Hebrews 2:11, 13).

Recall the discussion earlier where it is contended that it is very likely that, as physical sons grow in stature and maturity to become physical fathers themselves, so will spiritual sons such as Jesus Christ and the saints grow in the spirit realm to become spiritual Fathers someday. The analogies between the physical and spiritual realms are unmistakable.

13. WE ARE SENT TO EARTH BY THE FATHER.

Jesus Christ

"No one can come to Me unless the Father who sent Me draws him ..." (John 6:44).

"I came forth from the Father and have come into the world. Again, I leave the world and go to the Father" (John 16:28).

"... Jesus, knowing that the Father had given all things into His hand, and that He had come from God and was going to God ..." (John 13:3).

The Elect

"It is written in the prophets, 'And they shall all be taught by God' [Isaiah 54:13]. Therefore everyone who has heard and learned from the Father comes to Me" (John 6:45).

"And again: 'Here am I and the children whom God has given Me.' Inasmuch then as the children have partaken of flesh and blood, He Himself likewise shared in the same ..." (Hebrews 2:13-14).

14. WE WILL REIGN WITH THE FATHER ON HIS THRONE.

Jesus Christ

"But I saw no temple in it, for the Lord God Almighty and the Lamb are its temple" (Revelation 21:22).

"... we have such a High Priest, who is seated at the right hand of the throne of the Majesty in the heavens ..." (Hebrews 8:1).

The Elect

"To him who overcomes I will grant to sit with Me on My throne, as I also overcame and sat down with My Father on His throne" (Revelation 3:21).

15. WE WILL BE WORSHIPED [ONLY GODS CAN BE WORSHIPED].

Jesus Christ

"For it is written: 'As I live, says the Lord, every knee shall bow to Me, and every tongue shall confess to God [Isaiah 45:23]'" (Romans 14:11).

"... that at the name of Jesus every knee shall bow, of those in heaven, and those on earth, and those under the earth ..." (Philippians 2:10).

"And as they went to tell His disciples, behold, Jesus met them, saying, 'Rejoice!' So they came and held Him by the feet, and worshiped Him" (Matthew 28:9).

"And Jesus said unto him, 'You have both seen Him, and it is He who talks with you.' Then he said, 'Lord, I believe! And he worshiped Him" (John 9:37-38).

The Elect

"Indeed, I will make those of the synagogue

of Satan, who say they are Jews, and are not, but lie —indeed I will make them to come and worship before your [the saints'] feet, and to know that I have loved you" (Revelation 3:9).

"Kings shall be your foster fathers, and their queens your nursing mothers; they shall bow down to you with their faces to the earth, and lick up the dust of your feet. Then you will know that I am the Lord ..." (Isaiah 49:23).

"Also the sons of those who afflicted you shall come bowing to you, and all those who despised you shall fall prostrate at the soles of your feet ..." (Isaiah 60:14).

16. WE PRAY DIRECTLY TO THE FATHER.

Photo from *www.goodshepherd-protea.org*.

Jesus Christ

"Jesus spoke these words, lifted up His eyes to heaven, and said: 'Father, the hour has come'" (John 17:1).

"He went a little farther and fell on His face, and prayed, saying, 'O my Father, if it is possible, let this cup pass from Me; nevertheless, not as I will but as You will'" (Matthew 26:39).

The Elect

"In this manner, therefore, pray: Our Father in heaven, hallowed be Your name" (Matthew 6:9).

"But you, when you pray, go into your room, and when you have shut your door, pray to your Father who is in the secret place; and your Father who sees in secret will reward you openly" (Matthew 6:6).

17. THE FATHER SPEAKS DIRECTLY TO US.

Jesus Christ

"And suddenly a voice came from heaven, saying, 'This is My beloved Son, in whom I am well pleased'" (Matthew 3:17).

"While he was still speaking, behold, a bright cloud overshadowed them; and suddenly a voice came out of the cloud, saying, 'This is My beloved Son, in whom I am well pleased. Hear Him!'" (Matthew 17:5).

The Elect

God the Father speaks to the elect through the Word, the Scriptures.

"All scripture is given by inspiration of God, and is profitable for doctrine, for reproof, for correction, for instruction in righteousness ..." (II Timothy 3:16).

"And take the helmet of salvation, and the sword of the Spirit, which is the word of God ..." (Ephesians 6:17).

18. WE ENDURE TRIALS, SUFFER, AND OVERCOME AS LIVING SACRIFICES.

Jesus Christ

"For we do not have a High Priest who cannot sympathize with our weaknesses, but was in all points tempted as we are, yet without sin" (Hebrews 4:15).

"To him who overcomes I will grant to sit with Me on My throne, as I also overcame and sat down with My Father on His throne" (Revelation 4:21).

"If his offering is a burnt sacrifice of the herd, let him offer a male without blemish [typifying Jesus Christ]; he shall offer it of his own free will at the door of the tabernacle of meeting before the Lord" (Leviticus 1:3, and similar references elsewhere).

"He is despised and rejected of men, a man of sorrows and acquainted with grief. And we hid as it were, our faces from Him; He was despised, and we did not esteem Him. Surely He has borne our griefs, and carried our sorrows; yet we esteemed Him stricken, smitten by God, and afflicted. But He was wounded for our transgressions, He was bruised for our iniquities; the chastisement of our peace was upon Him, and by His stripes we are healed" (Isaiah 53:3-5; see also I Peter 2:21-24).

"... and when he [Pilate] had scourged Jesus, he delivered Him to be crucified.... And they [the soldiers] stripped Him, and put a scarlet robe on Him. When they had twisted a crown of thorns, they put it on His head .... Then they crucified Him ..." (Matthew 27:26, 28-29, 35).

The Elect

"... and if children, then heirs — heirs of God and joint heirs with Christ, if indeed we suffer with Him, that we may also be glorified together. For I consider that the sufferings of this present time are not worthy to be compared with the glory which shall be revealed in us" (Romans 8:17-18).

"In this you greatly rejoice, though now for a little while, if need be, you have been grieved by various trials, that the genuineness of your faith, being much more precious than gold that perishes, though it is tested by fire, may be found to praise, honor, and glory at the revelation of Jesus Christ" (I Peter 1:6-7).

"He who overcomes shall inherit all things, and I will be his God and he shall be My son" (Revelation 21:7).

"I beseech you therefore brethren, by the mercies of God, that you present your bodies a living sacrifice, holy, acceptable unto God, which is your reasonable service" (Romans 12:1).

"I have been crucified with Christ; it is no longer I who live, but Christ lives in me; and the life which I now live in the flesh I live by the faith of the Son of God, who loved me, and gave Himself for me" (Galatians 2:20).

19. WE ARE MINISTERED TO BY ANGELS.

Jesus Christ

"Then the devil left Him, and behold, angels came and ministered to Him" (Matthew 4:11).

"… 'Father, if it is Your will, take this cup from Me; nevertheless not My will, but Yours, be done.' Then an angel appeared to Him from heaven, strengthening Him" (Luke 22:42-43).

The Elect

"But to which of the angels has He ever said, 'Sit at My right hand, till I make Your enemies Your footstool'? Are they not all ministering spirits sent forth to minister for those who will inherit salvation?" (Hebrews 1:13-14).

"Do not forget to entertain strangers, for by so doing some have unwittingly entertained angels" (Hebrews 13:2).

20. WE FORGIVE THE SINS OF OTHERS.

Jesus Christ

"When Jesus saw their faith, He said to the paralytic, 'Son, be of good cheer; your sins are forgiven you.' And at once some of the scribes said within themselves, 'This Man blasphemes!', But Jesus, knowing their thoughts, said, 'Why do you think evil in your hearts? For which is easier to say, "Your sins are forgiven you," or to say, "Arise, and walk?" But that you may know that the Son of man has power on earth to forgive sins,' —then He said to the paralytic, 'Arise, take up you bed, and go to your house'" (Matthew 9:2-6; also in Mark 2:3-12 and Luke 5:18-26).

"Father, forgive them; for they know not what they do" (Luke 23:34).

"If we confess our sins, He is faithful and just to forgive us our sins and to cleanse us from all unrighteousness" (I John 1:9).

"I write unto you, little children, because your sins are forgiven you for His name's sake" (I John 2:12).

"For You, Lord, are good, and ready to forgive; and abundant in mercy unto all those who call upon You" (Psalm 86:5).

The Elect

"And forgive us our debts, as we forgive our debtors…. For if you forgive men their trespasses, your heavenly Father will also forgive you. But if you do not forgive men their trespasses, neither will your father forgive your trespasses" (Matthew 6:12, 14-15).

"So My heavenly Father also will do to you if each of you, from his heart, does not forgive his brother his trespasses" (Matthew 18:35).

"And whenever you stand praying, if you have anything against anyone, forgive him, that your Father in heaven may also forgive you your trespasses. But if you do not forgive, neither will your Father in heaven forgive your trespasses" (Mark 11:25-26).

"... forgive, and you shall be forgiven" (Luke 6:37).

"Take heed to yourselves. If your brother trespass against you, rebuke him; and if he repents, forgive him. And if he sins against you seven times in a day, and seven times in a day returns to you, saying, 'I repent,' you shall forgive him" (Luke 17:3-4).

"Now whom you forgive anything, I also forgive. For if indeed I have forgiven anything, I have forgiven that one for your sakes in the presence of Christ" (II Corinthians 2:10).

21. CHRIST AND THE ELECT ARE EQUIVALENT AT THE RESURRECTION.

Jesus Christ made no distinction between Himself and Mary at the tomb after His resurrection. He stated, "I ascend unto My Father and your Father; and to My God, and your God" (John 20:17). A special point was made to emphasize that He considered Himself no greater than one of the brethren in terms of the true Parent for each of us. He considered Himself, in fact, a part of the brethren by this declaration.

Besides, He acknowledged that the true Parent of each of us is the Father, and the only wellspring of hope we have — just as He had — is the resurrection from the dead to eternal life.

The Greek words used in John 20:17 for Father and God are as follows:

Father (Strong 3962) = *pater*, a father (lit. or fig., near or more remote).

God (Strong 2316) = *theos*, a deity, esp. the supreme Divinity, fig. a magistrate.

"For if we believe that Jesus died and rose again, even so God [the Father] will bring with Him those who sleep in Jesus" (I Thessalonians 4:14).

"Beloved, now we are children of God; and it has not yet been revealed what we shall be, but we know that when He is revealed, we shall be like Him, for we shall see Him as He is" (I John 3:2).

"... who [Christ] will transform our lowly body that it may be conformed to His glorious body, according to the working by which He is able even to subdue all things to Himself" (Philippians 3:21).

"But we all, with unveiled face, beholding as in a mirror the glory of the Lord, are being transformed into the same image from glory to glory, just as by the spirit of the Lord" (II Corinthians 3:18).

"For whom He foreknew, He also predestined to be conformed to the image of His Son, that He might be the first born among many brethren" (Romans 8:29).

"And as we have borne the image of
the man of dust, we shall also bear
the image of the heavenly Man"
(I Corinthians 15:49).

"... by which have been given to us
exceedingly great and precious promises,
that through these you may be partakers
of the divine nature, having escaped the
corruption that is in the world through
lust" (II Peter 1:4).

22. **THE LAW IS WRITTEN IN OUR
HEARTS, WE DO THE FATHER'S
WILL, AND WE HAVE HIS MIND.**

Jesus Christ

"Then answered Jesus and said unto them,
'Most assuredly, I say to you, the Son can
do nothing of Himself, but what He sees
the Father do; for whatever He does, the
Son also does in like manner'" (John 5:19).

"That they all may be one, as You, Father, are
in Me, and I in You, that they also may be
one in Us, that the world may believe that
You sent Me" (John 17:21).

"The Lord is well pleased for His
righteousness' sake; He will exult the law,
and make it honorable" (Isaiah 42:21).

"Do not think that I came to destroy the Law
or the Prophets. I did not come to destroy
but to fulfill. For assuredly, I say to you,
till heaven and earth pass away, one jot or
one tittle will by no means pass from the
law till all is fulfilled" (Matthew 5:17-18).

"But this shall be the covenant that I will
make with the house of Israel after those
days, says the Lord: I will put My law in
their minds, and write it on their hearts;
and I will be their God, and they shall be
My people" (Jeremiah 31:33).

The commandments and fruits of the spirit
codify for God's way of love to God and
love to one's neighbor (Exodus 20:2-17;
Galatians 5:22-23; Matthew 22:36-40).

The Elect

"Your kingdom come. Your will be done on
earth as it is in heaven" (Matthew 6:10).

"For who has known the mind of the Lord
that he may instruct Him? But we have
the mind of Christ"
(I Corinthians 2:16).

"Let this mind be in you which was also in
Christ Jesus" (Philippians 2:5).

"And it shall come to pass in the last days,
says God, that I will pour out of My
spirit upon all flesh; your sons and your
daughters shall prophesy, your young
men shall see visions, your old men shall
dream dreams, and on My menservants
and on My maidservants I will pour out
My spirit in those days; and they shall
prophesy" (Acts 2:17-18).

"But you are not in the flesh but in the
spirit, if indeed the spirit of God dwells
in you. Now if anyone does not have
the spirit of Christ, he is not His. And if
Christ is in you, the body is dead because

of sin, but the spirit is life because of righteousness" (Romans 8:9-10; righteousness is defined as keeping the commandments in Psalm 119:172).

23. WE ARE GIVEN A NAME THAT NO ONE ELSE KNOWS.

Jesus Christ

"His eyes were like a flame of fire, and on His head were many crowns. He had a name written that no man knew, except Himself" (Revelation 19:12).

The Elect

"He that has an ear, let him hear what the Spirit says unto the churches. To him that overcomes I will give some of the hidden manna to eat. And I will give him a white stone, and on the stone a new name written which no one knows except him who receives it" (Revelation 2:17).

24. WE ARE TO BE EXAMPLES OF GODLY LIVING TO THE WORLD.

Photo from Paul W. Syltie photo archives.

Jesus Christ

"Then answered Jesus and said unto them, 'Most assuredly, I say to you, the Son can do nothing of Himself, but what He sees the Father do; for whatever He does, the Son also does in like manner'" (John 5:19).
"I can of Myself do nothing. As I hear, I judge; and My judgment is righteous, because I do not seek My own will but the will of the Father who sent Me" (John 5:30).
"I must work the works of Him that sent Me while it is day; the night is coming when no one can work" (John 9:4).
"For I have not spoken on My own authority; but the Father who sent Me gave Me a command, what I should say and what I should speak" (John 12:49).
"Do you not believe that I am in the Father, and the Father in Me? The words that I speak to you I do not speak on My own authority; but the Father who dwells in Me does the works" (John 14:10).

The Elect

"For to this you were called, because Christ also suffered for us, leaving us an example, that you should follow His steps: Who committed no sin, nor was deceit found in His mouth, who when He was reviled, did not revile in return; when He suffered He did not threaten, but committed Himself to Him who judges righteously …" (I Peter 2:21-23).
"He who says he abides in Him ought himself also to walk just as He walked" (I John 2:6).
"Do not love the world or the things in the world. If anyone loves the world, the love of the Father is not in him. For all that is in the world — the lust of the flesh, the lust of the eyes, and the pride

of life — is not of the Father but is of the world. And the world is passing away, and the lust of it; but he who does the will of God abides forever" (I John 2:15-17).

"Come to Me, all you who labor and are heavy laden, and I will give you rest. Take My yoke upon you and learn from Me, for I am gentle and lowly in heart, and you will find rest for your souls. For My yoke is easy and My burden is light" (Matthew 11:28-30).

"For I have given you an example, that you should do as I have done to you" (John 13:15).

25. THERE IS HOPE OF GREAT GLORY IN THE SPIRIT REALM AFTER PHYSICAL DEATH

Jesus Christ

"... looking unto Jesus, the author and finisher of our faith, who for the joy that was set before Him endured the cross, despising the shame, and has sat down at the right hand of the throne of God" (Hebrews 12:2).
joy = *chara*, "cheerfulness, i.e. calm delight."

The Elect

"For I consider that the sufferings of this present time are not worthy to be compared with the glory which shall be revealed in us" (Romans 8:18).

"But as it is written: eye has not seen, nor ear heard, nor have entered into the heart of man the things which God has prepared for those who love Him" (I Corinthians 2:9).

26. WE HAVE BEEN SENT INTO THE WORLD

Jesus Christ and The Elect

"As You sent Me into the world, I also have sent them into the world" (John 17:18).

27. WE ARE NOT OF THE WORLD

Jesus Christ and The Elect

"I have given them Your word; and the world has hated them because they are not of the world, just as I am not of the world .... They are not of the world, just as I am not of the world" (John 17:14, 16).

28. WE ARE TEMPTED WITH EVIL

Jesus Christ

"For we do not have a High Priest who cannot sympathize with our weaknesses, but was in all points tempted as we are, yet without sin" (Hebrews 4:15).

The Elect

"Blessed is the man who endures temptation; for when he has been approved, he will receive the crown of life which the Lord has promised to those who love Him .... But each one is tempted when he is drawn away by his own desires and enticed" (James 1:12, 14).

29. WE WERE ORDAINED BEFORE THE FOUNDATION OF THE WORLD TO BE SONS OF GOD

Jesus Christ

"He [Jesus Christ] indeed was foreordained before the foundation of the world, but was manifest in these last times for you" (I Peter 1:20).

"In the beginning was the Word, and the Word was with God, and the Word was God. He was in the beginning with God …. And the Word became flesh and dwelt among us …" (John 1:1-2, 14).

The Elect

"Blessed be the God and Father of our Lord Jesus Christ, who has blessed us with every spiritual blessing in the heavenly places in Christ, just as He chose us in Him before the foundation of the world, that we should be holy and without blame before Him in love, having predestined us to adoption as sons by Jesus Christ to Himself, according to the good pleasure of His will, to the praise of the glory of His grace, by which He made us accepted in the Beloved" (Ephesians 1:3-6).

"For whom He foreknew He also predestined to be conformed to the image of His Son, that He might be the firstborn among many brethren. Moreover, whom He predestined these He also called; whom He called these He also justified; and whom He justified these He also glorified" (Romans 8:29-30).

"Now when the Gentiles heard this, they were glad and glorified the word of the Lord. And as many as had been *appointed* [*tasso* = 'to place in order, appoint'] to eternal life believed" (Acts 13:48).

30. WE WERE MADE A LITTLE LOWER THAN THE ANGELS

Jesus Christ

"But we see Jesus, who was made a little [while] lower than the angels, for the suffering of death crowned with glory and honor, that He, by the grace of God, might taste death for everyone" (Hebrews 2:9).

The Elect

"When I consider Your heavens, the work of Your fingers, the moon and the stars, which You have ordained, what is man that you are mindful of him, and the son of man that you visit him? For you have made him a little [while] lower than the angels, and You have crowned him with glory and honor. You have made him to have dominion over the works of Your hands; you have put all things under his feet …" (Psalm 8:3-6).

Here we see that both Jesus and the elect have been made lower than the spirit plane for "a little while," meaning that they are on equal terms in this sense, both flesh and blood which can die. Jesus Christ came from the spirit realm, where he preexisted, and lived as a human being in the image of Elohim just as the physical descendants of Adam have been doing for about 6,000 years. Jesus has been raised from the dead, the "firstborn of many brethren" (Romans 8:29), and the elect will be raised at the resurrection and likewise be given eternal life (I Thessalonians 4:16-17).

31. WE WILL BE RAISED BY THE SPIRIT OF THE FATHER IN US

Jesus Christ and The Elect

"But if the Spirit of Him who raised Jesus from the dead dwells in you, He who raised Christ from the dead will also give life to your mortal bodies through His spirit which dwells in you" (Romans 8:11). We are well aware that we, as saints, will be raised to eternal life at the resurrection, and be with the Father and Jesus Christ forever (I Thessalonians 4:13-17; Revelation 20:4). This is the same promise given to Jesus Christ, who is presently at the Father's right hand (Acts 2:33; Romans 8:34; Luke 22:69; I Peter 3:22), where the saints will also be after being raised (Revelation 3:21).

32. WE ARE JOINT HEIRS OF SALVATION

Jesus Christ and The Elect

"The Spirit itself bears witness with our spirit that we are children of God, and if children, then heirs — heirs of God and joint heirs with Christ, if indeed we suffer with Him, that we may also be glorified together" (Romans 8:16-17).

Of special interest is II Corinthians 3:18:
"But all of us who are Christians have no veils on our faces, but reflect like mirrors the glory of the Lord. We are transfigured in ever-increasing splendor into His own image, and the transformation comes from the Lord who is the spirit" (Phillips translation).

33. Spiros Zodhiates (editor), *The Complete Word Study New Testament*, AMG Publishers, Chattanooga, Tennessee, 1991, page 37 of the Greek Dictionary of the New Testament.

34. Spiros Zodhiates (editor), *The Complete Word Study New Testament*, AMG Publishers, Chattanooga, Tennessee, 1991, page 48 of the Greek Dictionary of the New Testament.

35. Picture from *www.gardeningknowhow.com*.

The Fifth Branch: Love Is Living His Government

1. Spiros Zodhiates (editor), *The Complete Word Study New Testament*, AMG

Publishers, Chattanooga, Tennessee, 1991, page 44 (*lordship = kyrieuo*), page 30 (*authority over = exousiazo*), page 40 (*lordship = katakurieou*), and page 41 (*authority = katexousiazo*) of the Greek Dictionary of the New Testament.

2. Genesis 3:22-24.

3. The population at the time of the Flood in Noah's day is unknown, but using the calculations of *bibliscienceguy.wordpress. com/2014/06/18/4-population-growth-how-many-died-in-noahs-flood/,* there could have been as many as 10 trillion people living at the time of the Flood. Here are the calculations.

"I'm now ready to calculate an estimate of how much the population grew from Adam and Eve to the Flood in 1656 years. I assume an average lifespan of 900 years, an average of 10 children per family averaging 5 boys and 5 girls that grow to adulthood and marry, 18 generations on average in family lines, and 10 generations in an average life span. Most of these estimates are probably pretty good except for the average number of children in a family, which I think was probably much higher. But these estimates will enable me to calculate a conservative lower bound for the Flood population.

"Using the third population formula included below (in bold), these parameters (P=2, c=5, g=18, k=10) yield a population of 9,536,742,187,500. To this must be added the unmarried childless people who were alive at the time. A very conservative estimate for this is 8% of the reproducing population. This gives a total **estimated population at the Flood of 10,299,681,562,500.** This is over **10 trillion** people! It corresponds to a **growth rate of 1.783%.** And I believe this estimate is low, since I used conservative estimates for the parameters.

"This estimated pre-Flood population of 10 trillion is another indication that the Flood was worldwide. The Flood would have to be global to destroy such a huge number of people. This estimated pre-Flood population of **10 trillion people** is well over 1,000 times today's world population of 7.1 billion people. How could this be possible? **Is 10 trillion a reasonable estimate for the population at the Flood?**" [Interested parties can review the formulas and math on the website above.]

4. Genesis 7:13.

5. *Book of Jasher* 7:29 through chapter 11.

6. Picture from *www.godswarplan.com.*

7. Picture from *www.thetorah.com.*

8. Genesis 11:7-8.

9. Read about Abram's early life and run-ins with Nimrod in *www.chabad.org.*

10. Genesis 12:1-5; Hebrews 11:8-10.

11. For the whole story, see Genesis 21 to 39.

12. This fascinating history is revealed in Genesis 47 to 50, and in Exodus, Leviticus, Numbers, Deuteronomy, and Joshua 1 to 5.

13. Photo from *www.freebibleimages.org*.
14. This history of Israel and Judah is covered in Samuel, Kings, Chronicles, and in the various prophetic books of the Old Testament, as well as in many historical references covering this period.
15. The history of Israel and Judah as they escaped captivity from Babylon and Assyria, and migrated north and west, can be traced through archaeological studies of Europe and Asia, as revealed in many sources such as those of Steven Collins: *Israel's Lost Empires (The Lost Tribes of Israel), Parthia: the Forgotten Ancient "Superpower" and Its Role in Biblical History, The "Lost" Ten Tribes of Israel … Found!, Israel's Tribes Today,* and *Origins and Empire of Ancient Israel (The Lost Tribes of Israel)*.
16. See the books of Ezra and Nehemiah.
17. See the accounts of the crucifixion and resurrection in Matthew 27:26-66, Mark 15:15-47, Luke 23:24-56. and John 19:16-42.
18. Acts 2 and 3.
19. Luke 12:32.
20. Colossians 1:26.
21. Galations 5:1; I Corinthians 8:9; II Corinthians 3:17; John 8:36; James 1:25.
22. *www.infographicfacts.com*.
23. Pictures from *www.pocketmags.com* (Stalin), *www.history.com* (Hitler), *www.gqindia.com* (Fidel Castro), and *www.thoughtco.com* (Idi Amin).
24. Michael Agnes (editor), *Webster's New World College Dictionary*, Fourth Edition, Wiley Publishing, Inc., Cleveland, Ohio, 2004, page 614.
25. Picture from *www.lonelyplanet.com*.
26. See 1, page 54.
27. See 1, page 33.
28. See 1, pages 54 and 55.
29. See 1, page 62.
30. See 1, page 22.
31. Picture from *www.dreamcatcherreality.com*.
32. See 1, page 31.
33. See 1, Page 44.
34. See 1, page 58.
35. Picture from *www.am630theword.com*.

The Sixth Branch: Love Is the Least Being Greatest, and the Last First
1. Picture from *www.pijingoo.wordpress.com*.
2. Picture from *www.jw.org*.
3. Spiros Zodhiates (editor), *The Complete Word Study New Testament*, AMG Publishers, Chattanooga, Tennessee, 1991, page 77 of the Greek Dictionary of the New Testament.
4. Picture from *www.hub.jhu.edu*.
5. Picture from *www.stmichaellivermore.com*.
6. See 1, page 38.
7. See 1, page 51.
8. See 1, page 49.
9. Picture from *www.jw.org*.
10. See 1, page 70.
11. Picture from Laurence J. Peter, *The Peter*

Pyramid, William Morrow and Company, 1986.

12. Picture from *www.pinterest.com.*
13. A.R. Fausset, *A Commentary On the Old and New Testaments, Volume 2,* William B. Eerdmans Publishing Company, Grand Rapids, Michigan, 1973, page 335.
14. F.C. Eiselen, E. Lewis, and D.G. Downey, *The Abingdon Bible Commentary,* Abingdon Press, Nashville, Tennessee, 1929, page 740.
15. F. C. Cook, *Barnes' Notes, Commentary on Proverbs, Ecclesiastes, Song of Solomon, Jeremiah, Ezekiel,* Baker Book House, Grand Rapids, Michigan, 1879, page 390.

The Seventh Branch: Love Is the Foundation of Marriage

1. Rose Michaels (pseudonym for a writer living in Ohio), *Christianity Today International/Marriage Partnership,* Fall 2004, Vol. 21, No. 3, page 58.
2. Picture from *www.jw.org,* How to stop strife in the home.
3. Picture from the author.
4. Warren Baker (editor), *The Complete Word Study Old Testament,* AMG Publishers, Chattanooga, Tennessee, 1994, page 60 *(laqach),* page 86 *(ownah),* page 45 *(chathan),* and page 22 *(baal)* of the Hebrew and Chaldee Dictionary.
5. Spiros Zodhiates (editor), *The Complete Word Study New Testament,* AMG Publishers, Chattanooga, Tennessee, 1991,
page 20 *(gameo* and *ginomai)* and page 26 *(ekgamizo)* of the Greek Dictionary of the New Testament.
6. See 3, page 9 *(ohab* and *ahabah).*
7. See 4, page 76 *(storge),* page 75 *(philautos),* and page 50 *(xenia).*
8. Picture from *www.seedsoffaith.cph.org.*
9. See 5, page 42
10. See 5, page 76.
11. Picture from *www.stellartransport.com.*
12. See 4, page 117.
13. See 4, page 51.
14. See 4, page 72.
15. See 4, page 108.
16. Picture from the author.
17. See 4, page 75.
18. See 5, page 59.
19. See 5, page 31.
20. Picture from *www.commons.wikimedia.org.*
21. Anonymous, Migration and Modern Slavery, Pornography, *www.justfreedom.org.*
22. Isaac Wolf, Child porn industry using web-based system to move funds, *www.eastvalleytribune.com.*
23. Picture from the author.
24. Viktor E. Frankl, *Man's Search for Meaning, An Introduction to Logotherapy,* Third Edition, A Touchstone Book, 1984, page 116. Dr. Frankl states his case about love in marriage by integrating the meanings of love as follows: "Love is the only way to grasp another human being in the innermost core of his personality. No one can become fully aware of the very presence

of another human being unless he loves him. By this love he is enabled to see the essential traits and features in the beloved person; and even more, he sees that which is potential in him, which is not yet actualized but yet ought to be actualized. Furthermore, by his love the loving person enables the beloved person to actualize these potentialities. By making him aware of what he can be and of what he should become, he makes these potentialities come true.

"In logotherapy, love is not interpreted as a mere epiphenomenon of sexual drives and instincts in the sense of a so-called sublimation. Love is as primary a phenomenon as sex. Normally, sex is a mode of expression for love. Sex is justified, even sanctified, as soon as, but only as long as, it is a vehicle for love. Thus love is not understood as a mere side-effect of sex; rather, sex is a way of expressing the experience of that ultimate togetherness which is called love."

The Eighth Branch: Love Is Revealed in the Creation

1. Brisbane News Group, Tank and Muck - Two canine heroes team up to save toddler, *Shining World Awards*, November 11, 2008, *www.award.godsdirectcontact.net*.
2. Anonymous, Dolphins save swimmers from shark attack, *News, sport and opinion from the Guardian's US edition,* *The Guardian.*
3. Picture from *www.theconversation.com*.
4. Amber Lee, Sea lion saves Golden Gate Bridge suicide jumper, survivor says $210 million net is crucial, July 12, 2019, *www.ktvu.com*.
5. Robert L. Pitman and John W. Durban, Save the seal! Whales act instinctively to save seals, *Natural History, Exploring Science and Nature,* November, 2009, *www.naturalhistorymag.com*.
6. Picture from *www.us.whales.org*.
7. Richard Grant, Do trees talk to each other?, *Smithsonian Magazine*, March, 2018, *www.smithsonianmag.com*.
8. Peter Wohlleben, *The Hidden Life of Trees: What They Feel, How They Communicate — Discoveries from a Secret World,* Greystone Books, 2016.
9. See 7.
10. See 8.
11. See 3.
12. Picture from *www.haarlemartspace.co.uk*.
13. Suzanne Simard, see 8.
14. Peter Tompkins and Christopher Bird, *The Secret Life of Plants,* Harper and Row, Publishers, 1989.
15. Soren J. Sorensen, Bacteria contradict Darwin: Survival of the friendliest, University of Copenhagen, *Science Daily,* December 11, 2019, *www.sciencedaily.com*.
16. Picture from *www.medicalnewstoday.com*.
17. See 15.
18. F. B. Dazzo and S. Ganter, Root exudation

and rhizodeposition in the rhizosphere, *Encyclopedia of Microbiology* (Third Edition), Academic Press, 2009, *www.sciencedirect.com.*

19. Paul W. Syltie, *How Soils Work*, Xulon Press, Fairfax, Virginia, 2002.

20. Anonymous, Benefits of mycorrhizae, Myke Pro, Mycorrhizal Inoculant, Premier Tech Ltd., *www.mykepro.com.*

21. Picture from the author.

22. Picture from *www.thinglink.com.*

23. John Young, Basic types of cells, *Untamed Science, www.untamedscience.com.*

24. Anonymous, The meaning of numbers: the number 12, *www.biblestudy.org.*

25. Katy McLaughlin, Body systems, October 19, 2020, *www.biologydictionary.net.*

26. Adam Felman, How does blood work, and what problems occur? *Medical News Today*, August 25, 2017, *www.medicalnewstoday.com.*

27. Kim Zimmerman, The circulatory system: an amazing circuit that keeps our bodies going, *Live Science*, August 8, 2019, *www.livescience.com.*

28. Joseph Mercola, Water Supports Health in Ways You May Never Have Suspected, January 28, 2017, *www.mercola.com.*

29. Picture from *www.quizlet.com.*

30. Cleveland Clinic, The structure and function of the digestive system, *www.my.clevelandclinic.org.*

31. Anonymous, Human microbiome, *en.wikipedia.org.*; Saurabh Sethi, What are the gut microbiota and human microbiome? *Medical News Today*, June 26, 2018, *www.medicalnewstoday.com.*

32. Kristen Ciccolini, If your gut could talk: 10 things you should know, *Healthline*, September 17, 2018, *www.healthline.com.*

33. Picture from *www.thoughtco.com.*

34. S. C. Freeman, Physiology, exocrine gland, October 1, 2020, *www.ncbi.nlm.nih.gov*; Anonymous, Endocrine system, *en.wikipedia.org.*

35. Anonymous, Immune system, *en.wikipedia.org.*

36. Picture from *www.canadalymph.ca.*

37. Anonymous, Lymphatic system: facts, functions, and diseases, *Live Science, www.livescience.com.*

38. Picture from *www.popularmechanics.com.*

39. Anonymous, Nervous system, *en.wikipedia.org.*

40. Kim Zimmerman, Nervous system: facts, function, and diseases, February 14, 2018, *www.livescience.com.*

41. Anonymous, What is the strongest muscle in the human body?, Library of Congress, *www.loc.gov.*

42. Ross Toro, Diagram of the human muscular system, August 20, 2013. *www.livescience.com.*

43. *www.bemarrahealth.com.*

44. Kim Zimmerman, Reproductive system: facts, functions, and diseases, March 22, 2018, *www.livescience.com.*

45. Anonymous, Your bones, *www.kidshealth.*

com; Anonymous, Human skeleton, *en.wikipedia.org.*

46. Picture from *www.livescience.com.*
47. Anonymous, Respiratory system, *en.wikipedia.org.*
48. See 46.
49. Anonymous, Urinary system, *en.wikipedia.org.*
50. Anonymous, Integumentary system, *en.wikipedia.org.*
51. For a good discussion on accommodation, see Alexis Carrel, *Man the Unknown,* Harper and Brothers, New York, 1935.
52. According to Michael Agnes (editor), *Webster's New World College Dictionary,* Fourth Edition, Wiley Publishing, Inc., Cleveland, Ohio, 2004, page 952, mutualism is "symbiosis with mutual advantage to both or all organisms involved."
53. Picture from *www.today.com.*

The Ninth Branch: Love Is the Granting of Health and Fulfillment

1. Picture from *www.dailycaring.com.*
2. Doc G, Earn and Invest, Money can't buy health, August 7, 2018, *www.diversefi.com.*
3. Spiros Zodhiates (editor), *The Complete Word Study New Testament,* AMG Publishers, Chattanooga, Tennessee, 1991, page 57 of the Greek Dictionary of the New Testament.
4. Picture from the author.
5. See 3, page 33.
6. See 3, page 73.
7. Warren Baker (editor), *The Complete Word Study Old Testament,* AMG Publishers, Chattanooga, Tennessee, 1994, page 114 of the Hebrew and Chaldee Dictionary; Shawn Brasseaux, What is the "botch of Egypt?" *www.forwhatsaiththescriptures.org.*
8. See 7, page 45.
9. See 7, page 83.
10. See 7, page 43.
11. Picture from *www.jw.org.*
12. Anonymous, Hepatitis E, World Health Organization, July 27, 2020, *www.who.int;* Coral Beach, Scientists find cause for concern about hepatitis E in slaughterhouse pigs, *Food Safety News, www.foodsafetynews.com;* Denise Minger, *Healthline,* June 22, 2017, *www.healthline.com.*
13. Denise Minger, *Healthline,* June 22, 2017, *www.healthline.com.*
14. See 13.
15. See 13.
16. Sara Ipatenco, *http://www.livestrong.com;* Anonymous, Diseases in pork, *www.wikipedia.org.*
17. See 16.
18. Picture from *www.canr.msu.edu.*
19. See 16.
20. Anonymous, The dangers of eating raw shellfish, *www.ny.gov;* Martha Iwamoto et. al., Epidemiology of seafood-associated infections in the United States, *Clinical*

Microbiology Reviews, April 23, 2010, 399-411.

21. See 20.

22. Warren Baker (editor), *The Complete Word Study Old Testament*, AMG Publishers, Chattanooga, Tennessee, 1994, page 101 of the Hebrew and Chaldee Dictionary.

23. Picture from *http://www.biblestudytools.com*.

24. Anonymous, Sexually transmitted infections (STIs), *www.wikipedia.org*; Anonymous, What are HIV and AIDS? *www.hiv.gov*.

25. Picture from *www.letterpile.com*.

26. See 22, page 78.

27. See 22, page 113.

28. Eric Olson, Lack of sleep: can it make you sick? Mayo Clinic Patient Care and Health Information, *www.mayoclinic.org*; Jill Thompson, Surprising link between sleep deprivation and mental illnesses (psychosis), *Sleep Advisor*, June 5, 2018, *www.sleepadvisor.org*.

29. Picture from *www.barnstablecountyhealth.org*.

30. S.I. McMillen, *None of These Diseases,* Fleming H. Revell Company, Old Tappan, New Jersey, 1963.

31. See 30.

32. See 3, page 48.

33. Louis Terrance, *www.change.org*.

34. M. Rosie Shrout and Daniel Weigel, Infidelity's aftermath: Appraisals, mental health, and health-compromising behaviors following a partner's infidelity, *Journal of Social and Personal Relationships,* April 21, 2017.

35. See 3, page 31.

36. See 30.

37. Chris Kresser, 10 ways refined flour can damage your health, April 16, 2019, *www. chriskresser.com*; Anonymous, GMO Facts, *www.nongmoproject.org*.

38. Picture from *www.eatthis.com*.

39. Gina Roberts-Grey, The truth is, lying makes you sick, *Next Avenue*, August 28, 2012, *www.nextavenue.org*.

40. See 22, page 40.

41. Ian York, What would happen biologically if someone drank blood? How would it be processed in the body? *Quora*, March 10, 2013, *www.quora.com*; Anonymous, Animal fat, *www.nutritionfacts.org*

42. Eugenia Tognotti, Lessons from the History of Quarantine, from Plague to Influenza A, NCBI, *Emerging Infectious Diseases*, February, 2013, Volume 19(2): 254–259. doi: 10.3201/eid1902.120312.

43. Picture from *Eyesalve to See*, *www.safeguardyoursoul.com*.

44. See 22, page 110.

The Tenth Branch: Love Is the Fellowship of the Saints

1. Bob Gilliam, The importance of fellowship in a New Testament church, May 26, 2004, *www.bible.org*.

2. Picture from *www.chongsoonkim. blogspot.com*.

3. Spiros Zodhiates (editor), *The Complete*

Word Study New Testament, AMG Publishers, Chattanooga, Tennessee, 1991, page 42 of the Greek Dictionary of the New Testament.

4. See 3, page 54.
5. Warren Baker (editor), *The Complete Word Study Old Testament,* AMG Publishers, Chattanooga, Tennessee, 1994, page 102 of the Hebrew and Chaldee Dictionary.
6. See 5, page 89.
7. See 5, page 24.
8. See 5, page 102.
9. Picture from *www.history.com.*
10. See 3, page 62.
11. See 3, Page 22.
12. See 3, page 78 *(psalmos),* page 23 *(didache),* page 20 *(glossa),* page 14 *(apokalupsis),* and page 32 *(hermeneia).*
13. Picture from Elders, ordinations, and the laying on of hands, unpublished article by Paul W. Syltie, June 28, 2018.
14. See 3, page 60.

The Consequences of Failing to Practice Love

1. Rod Dreher, Our loveless world, *The American Conservative,* July 22, 2019, *www.theamericanconservative.com.*
2. Picture from the author.
3. Rolf Witzche, On the subject of nuclear physics and the Universe being a "miracle" on intention by a Mind that is Love, *Discovering Love,* Chapter 16, 2011, Christian Science God, *www.ice-age-ahead-iaa.ca/alternate_healing/2011christianscience/christian_science_god.html.*
4. Picture from *www.abc.net.au.*
5. Dewey B. Larson, *Nothing But Motion,* Volume 1 of a revised and enlarged edition of *The Structure of the Physical Universe,* North Pacific Publishers, Portland, Oregon, 1959.
6. See 5.
7. See 5.
8. Declaration of Independence: a Transcription, In Congress, July 4, 1776, America's founding documents, National Archives, *www.archives.gov.*
9. Picture from *www.archives.gov.*
10. Anonymous, U.S. Constitution ratified, This day in history, June 21, *History, www.history.com.*
11. Robert Smith, Computers and the Mark of the Beast, The core memory, *www.thecorememory.com*; Texe Marrs, *Project L.U.C.I.D.: The Beast 666 Universal Human Control System,* Living Truth Publishers, 1996.
12. George Orwell, *1984,* Secker and Warburg, 1949.
13. Anonymous, A world without love: the ramifications of an affectionless society in 1984, May 24, 20189, *www.gradesfixer.com.*
14. Picture from *www.arcgis.com.*
15. The Hegelian dialectic comprises three dialectical stages of development: a thesis, giving rise to its reaction, called an antithesis, which contradicts or

negates the thesis and the tension between the two is resolved by means of a synthesis. In more simplistic terms, one can consider it thus: problem → reaction → solution. The method is used to gradually move a person or group from one position to another as the dialectics follow one another. See Dialectic at *en.wikipedia.org*.

16. Picture from *www.radcliffeontrentww1.org.uk*.

17. Picture from the author, constructed by Abigail Evans, *www.abigailsyltieart.com*.

SUBJECT INDEX

SCRIPTURE INDEX

17:5	29, 31	27:36	46	12:21-22	25
17:20-21	XIII			13:8	38
17:20-23	15, 38	**ROMANS**		13:8-10	XVI, 76
17:21	72	1:12	46	15:2	XVI, 14
17:26	XVI	1:19-20	36, 79, 98		
21:17	XVII	1:28-31	38	**I CORINTHIANS**	
		2:6	54	1:26-29	52
ACTS		2:11	55	2:9-10	XV, 137, 138
2:33-34	31	2:17	54	2:9-11	35
2:38	X, 6, 14, 15	3:25	14	5:1-5	110
5:28	5	4:11-13	6, 8	5:1-13	74
5:31	31	4:15	110	7:9	69
7:49	58	5:6-8	20	7:10-11	70
7:55-56	31	5:8	XVI, 55	7:25-35	72
8:17-19	15	6:17-18	137	7:39	70, 74
10:34	55	6:23	54	8:6	58
10:38	110	7:3	69	11:3	68, 69
10:43	14	8:3	31	11:7	15
11:23	46	8:9	14	12	38, 45, 49, 97, 121
14:22	120	8:17	103	12:7	57
14:23	123	8:26-27	XII	12:12-27	97
15:32	120	8:29	6, 15, 28, 38, 47, 60	12:18	36, 45, 55
16:40	46, 120	8:29-30	30	13	14, 121
17:26	29	8:34	57	13:1-8	15, 45
17:30	15	8:36	21	13:13	XVII, 14
18:27	120	8:39	55	14	47, 121, 123
19:6	15	11:2	120	14:3	46
19:11-12	110	11:17-24	58	14:23-26	119
20:1	120	11:26	35	14:26	122
20:2	46	12:4-8	49	14:29	122
20:17	48	12:6-8	38, 45	14:31	120
20:28	48, 123	12:9-10	23, 38	14:39	123
20:29-30	48	12:17-21	XII, 46	14:40	122
21:25	115	12:19	25	15:20	20

CPSIA information can be obtained
at www.ICGtesting.com
Printed in the USA
BVHW011942310123
657546BV00005B/88